A Century of Handbags

The Modern Handbag for Antique Lovers

77 Lower Valley Road, Atglen, PA 19310

Kate Dooner

Printed in the United States of America.
ISBN: 0-88740-465-0

Published by Schiffer Publishing, Ltd.
77 Lower Valley Road
Atglen, PA 19310
Please write for a free catalog.
This book may be purchased from the publisher.
Please include $2.95 postage.
Try your bookstore first.

We are interested in hearing from authors
with book ideas on related subjects.

Contents

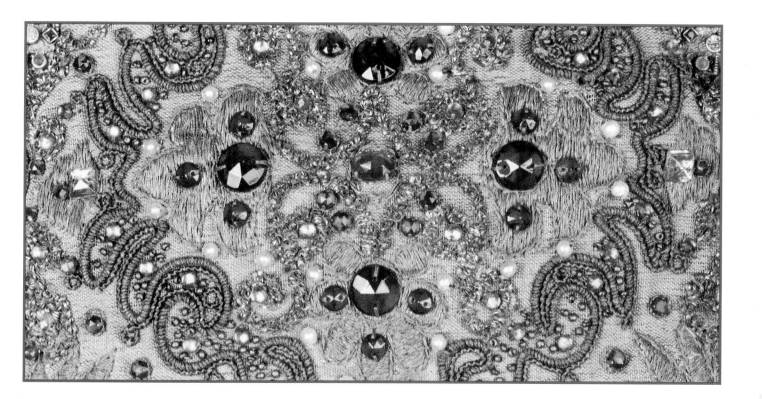

Acknowledgements

Thanks to all who allowed their handbags to appear in this book, including: Francine Cohen; Bootie Mitchie; Susan Spilkin; Dianne Rosenberg; Bess Goodson; Linnet Bolduc; Asprey, London; Classics Illustrated, William Goldberg; Veronica Manusis and Tanya Hunter, Cobra and Bellamy, London; Florence Geller, Piacente, Tarrytown, New York; Anne Hopkin; Kaylee Freedman; Katy Kane, New Hope, Pennsylvania; Margaret B. Schiffer; Margaret M. Nutt; Nancy Schiffer; Catherine Bonnet, Louis Vuitton; Janet Roller; Pierre Deux; Kathy Gallagher, Judith Leiber; Gary Franke and David Kratzer, Steppin' Out; Mim Klein; Matthew Burkholz, Route 66 Antiques, Chatham, New York; Larry Campbell, Radio Times; Roy Rover and Adrienne Lorber, New York City; and Peggy Ann Osborne.

$\mathcal{I}$ntroduction

The Handbag As We Know It Today

In centuries past, both men and women dangled small decorative drawstring bags from their belts. These functional pouches were known as aumoniéres and, for the most part, were used for carrying coins and other small essentials. At the end of the eighteenth century, they began to use the reticule, another type of drawstring bag. The handbag proper entered the scene at the end of the nineteenth century, when it was also used purely as a functional item.

The handbag as we know it today, however, is a phenomenon of the twentieth century. It has become an integral part of the fashion industry, influenced, as is all fashion, by cultural events and attitudes of the period. As the emancipation of women grew and as women started to work, the handbag became a permanent and necessary

Bargello wool needlepoint purse of red and green tones marked "1756, MM," folded in thirds, 6" x 4" and lined in blue silk.

fixture of the feminine wardrobe. While housebound women had the time and inclination to make their own bags in the nineteenth century, in the new era it became fashionable to purchase them —if possible, one for each outfit of the day. A bag used for tea in the afternoon would certainly not be appropriate for the evening's outing! Just as shoes had to be changed for each outfit, so did handbags.

The dawn of this new century ushered in a fresh attitude towards style, which did not fail to be reflected in handbags. The new style, Art Nouveau, relied little upon classical forms or outmoded symbols from the 1800s. Instead, it featured natural motifs, exotic decorative animals in settings of leaves and flowers, and flowing lines. The female form was lean, elongated, and swathed in sweeping gauze materials; hair was always long and flowing. Handbags of the Art Nouveau era (approximately 1900-1920) were decorated with many such designs.

The graceful Art Nouveau style was just the beginning of the modern handbag's exciting evolution. Through the Deco years of the twenties and thirties, the war years of the forties, the atomic fifties, the radical sixties, and the designer seventies and eighties, handbags grew increasingly ingrained in our culture. More than just an accessory, the handbag became a fashion statement.

Bargello wool needlepoint purse in red, yellow and blue tones and marked "I C, 1760," folded in thirds with green linen lining sewn as two interior pockets, 7" x 4.5".

Alligator medical style bag with single handle and silver locking clasp engraved JED and marked "Pat. Aug 19, 8-," 17" x 7".
Courtesy of Piacente

Alligator medical style bag with single grip handle marked with engraved initials J.C.Y. and 1894 written on the brass frame, 13.5'' x 8.5''. *Courtesy of Piacente*

Felt and alligator bag. 13'' x 10''. *Courtesy of Piacente*

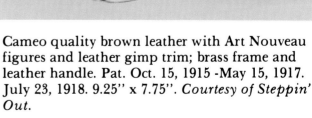

Cameo quality brown leather with Art Nouveau figures and leather gimp trim; brass frame and leather handle. Pat. Oct. 15, 1915 -May 15, 1917. July 23, 1918. 9.25'' x 7.75''. *Courtesy of Steppin' Out.*

Hand tooled leather bag, c. 1910. Marked, Basco Built. 9'' x 6''. *Courtesy of Classics Illustrated, William Goldberg.*

Japanese Kinchaku, 19th century. Enamel on sterling frame and woven thread design on cloth. 6.5'' x 5.5''. *Courtesy of Francine Cohen.*

Chapter 1

1920s—The Flapper Years

World War I was over, and the frantic, frivolous and youthful attitudes of the speakeasy '20s pervaded fashion just as they did the novels of Edith Wharton and F. Scott Fitzgerald. Picasso was in Paris with the Cubists shocking the high art world, while the decorative arts were flourishing with the sleek new Art Deco look of Erte and René Lalique. Classy, fashion-conscious women wore clothing modelled after the hip "flapper" looks —the ultimate in slim, waistless dresses, featuring strappy shoulders, feathers, long swinging faux pearls, and *never* enough fringe. They carried a variety of handbags: large leather bags, small beaded bags, the minaudière, and the chatelaine, a stylish pouch bag that attached to the belt. Fashion was crucial in this era; it announced to all spectators that a woman was elegant, classy, and, above all, modern.

In some ways, this "modernity" involved delving into the past —but never the recent past. As Hollywood reached the masses and the film industry became a part of American culture, every woman began to want for herself the medieval romance and glamour of women in such films as *El Cid, The Crusades* and *Joan of Arc.* In 1909, A.C.

 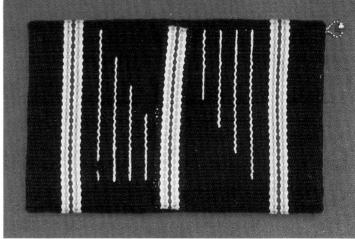

Chimayo, New Mexico bag woven by the Ortega family. Sterling silver clasp. 9" x 6". (front and back view). *Courtesy of Mim Klein.*

Chimayo, New Mexico bag, hand woven by the Ortega family. Sterling silver clasp. Tag reads, "El Grandee Fred Harvey" Arizona and New Mexico. 6.5" x 6". (front and back view). *Courtesy of Mim Klein.*

Chimayo bag, possibly by the Ortega family. Tag reads, "Hand woven, hand tailored in Santa Fe, New Mexico by Ganocraft made expressly for the Utah Parks Company." 13.75" x 11.75". *Courtesy of Mim Klein.*

Group of bags in architectural designs, c. 1925. In back, brown leather with chrome frame/handle marked "Genuine Morocco, Best London Make." 8" w. x 7" h. Left: black kid with chrome handle, ball catch and the initial "F". 8.25" w. x 6.5" h. Right: blue kid with chrome handle and initials "JAT." 11" w. x 8.5" h. The bag in front is unmarked. *Courtesy of Steppin' Out.*

Pratt had invented the mesh-making machine, just what the fashion industry would need to cater to this "knights and fair ladies" trend. By 1926, technical advances made it possible to produce a mesh so fine that its texture resembled fabric. White or pot metal chain was usually used, but fashions featuring German silver, sterling and other metals also appeared. Metal mesh bags were manufactured to match the many gold and silver frocks fashionable at the time.

These mesh bags were not new —they had been used since the eighteenth century. One of the first firms to manufacture handbags and decorative accessories of mesh in America was Whiting and Davis of Plainville, Massachusetts. It was founded in 1876 as Wade, Davis and Company and became Whiting and Davis when Whiting joined the firm in July, 1880. Known for their high quality, they made finely designed metal mesh purses with colorful Art Deco motifs throughout the 1920s. They are still in operation today.

Beaded bags, also popular during the 1920s, sported geometric patterns and abstract designs, and often were attached to celluloid frames. They were frequently made in Germany or Czechoslovakia with Bavarian, Bohemian or Muranese glass beads. Many beaded bags of the period were drawstring-type reticules ornamented with swag or shaggy bead fringe. Tabour, needlepoint and tapestry bags were also popular.

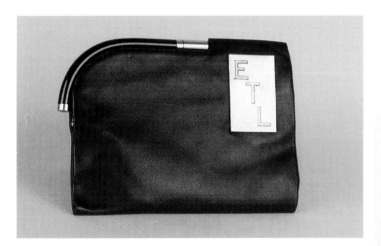

Black calf clutch with silver trim initialed "ETL," 1920s-1940s. Pat. # 17614 with black plastic and silver half-exposed frame. *Courtesy of Steppin' Out.*

Black leather and plastic handbag with change purse and mirror inside. *Courtesy of Cobra and Bellamy.*

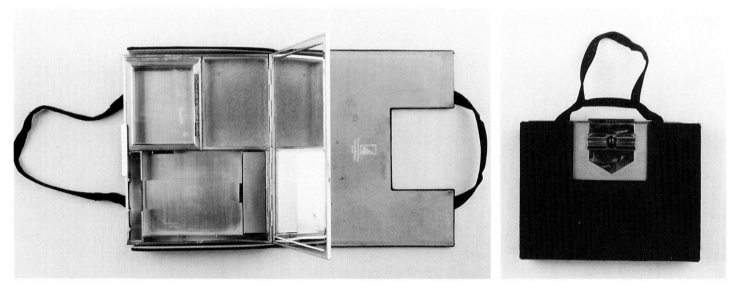

La minaudière de Van Cleef & Arpels, shown open and closed. *Courtesy of Cobra and Bellamy.*

Black and white silhouetted handbag with swan on one side and Buddhist temple on the other. *Courtesy of Cobra and Bellamy*

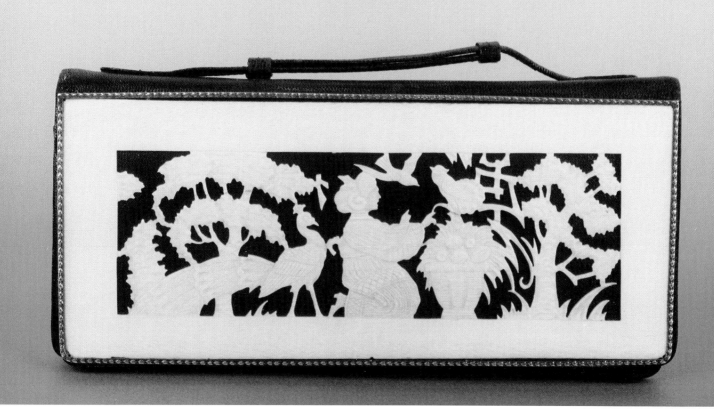

Hand-carved ivory with sterling silver frame on black pin-seal leather. 3.25'' x 7.5''. *Courtesy of Francine Cohen.*

Two beautiful tapestry handbags. *Courtesy of Asprey*

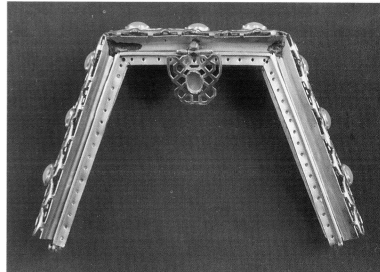

Ornate handbag frame. *Courtesy of Fior*

Sterling silver mesh bag by E.A.M., USA. *Courtesy of Linnet Bolduc.*

Gold mesh evening bag with rhinestone clip; cream-colored mesh evening bag; gold mesh billfold and coin purse; all by the Whiting and Davis Company. *Courtesy of Linnet Bolduc.*

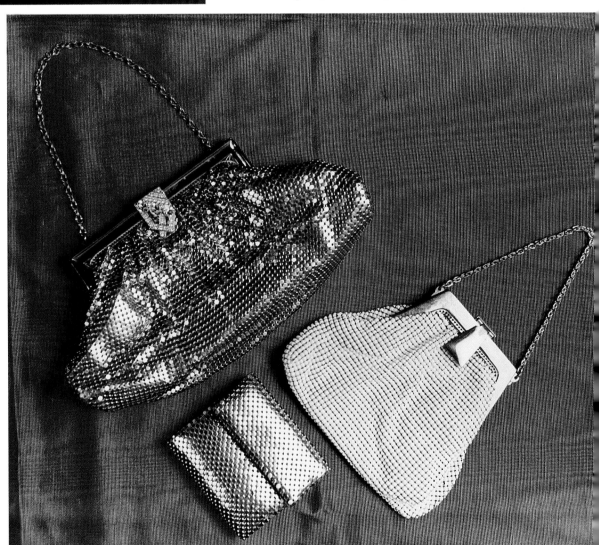

German Silver Mesh Bags.

(See Previous page for full description.)
Lined with white silk or white kid.

B27211	(5¼ inch)	$3.25 Each	
C27211	(6 inch)	$3.75 Each	
B27034	(5¼ inch)	$3.00 Each	
E27129	(2¾ inch)	$10.50 dozen (unlined)	
D21900	(3¾ inch)	$1.50 each (unlined)	
A27211	(4½ inch)	$2.75 Each	
C27034	(6 inch)	$3.50 Each	
A27034	(4½ inch)	$2.50 Each	
E27192	(2¾ inch)	$9.00 dozen (unlined)	

Any of our bags furnished with balls attached at 10 cents per bag extra.

German Silver Mesh Bags.
Pierced Frames.

27176 $12.00 each.   27177 $12.00. each.

Frames are beautifully pierced; also engraved.

They are unlined as the mesh is fine and strong and no lining is required. Note continuous wire method of attaching mesh to frame.

German Silver—Soldered Links.

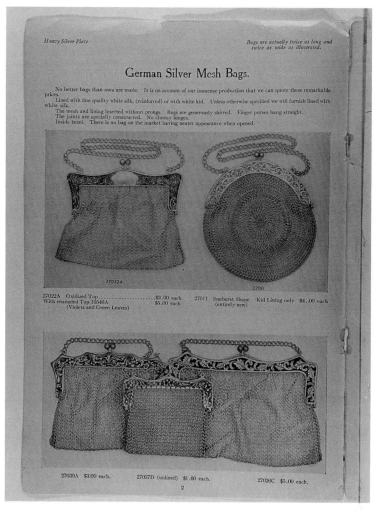

A27173 (Silk Lined) $6.75 each.   B27181 (unlined) $12.00 each.

Each link is soldered and bags are very strong.

German Silver Mesh Bags.

(See previous page for full description).
Lined with White Silk or White Kid.

C21948	$3.75 each	B21948		$3.25 each
A21948	2.75 "	A10562	Enameled Ornament	3.75 "
21900	2.00 "	B10562	Enameled Ornament	4.37 "
		C10562	Enameled Ornament	5.12 "

A24158 .... $3.75 Each

Furnished in B size at $3.00 and in C size at $5.50.
Set with best quality imitation stone—Jade or Turquoise.
State which is desired.

27117 Sterling Silver Front .... $3.25 Each

This bag has a Sterling Silver hand engraved front on the frame.
The balance is of German Silver as on other bags.

B27097—Discontinued.

German Silver Mesh Bags.

No better bags than ours are made. It is on account of our immense production that we can quote these remarkable prices.

Lined with fine quality white silk, (reinforced) or with white kid. Unless otherwise specified we will furnish lined with white silk.

The mesh and lining inserted without prongs. Bags are generously shirred. Finger purses hang straight.

The joints are specially constructed. No clumsy hinges.

Inside bezel. There is no bag on the market having neater appearance when opened.

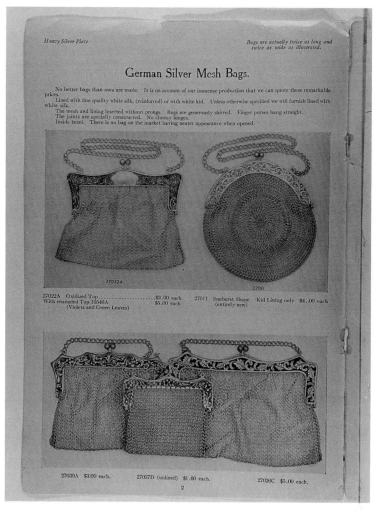

27022A Oxidized Top .... $3.00 each
With enameled Top 10546A .... $5.00 each
(Violets and Green Leaves)
27011 Sunburst Shape (entirely new) Kid Lining only $4.00 each

27039A $3.00 each.   27037D (unlined) $1.60 each.   27025C $5.00 each.

Elegant frame of chrysoprase and marcasites on
sterling made by Anton Moritz, Lexington Ave.,
New York. 7.5" x 8.5". *Courtesy of Francine
Cohen.*

Left: Hattie Carnegie bag marked, "Made in
France," with cut glass decorations, 6" x 8.5".
Right: Black onyx clasp on top and marcasites on
silver, 7" x 9". *Courtesy of Francine Cohen.*

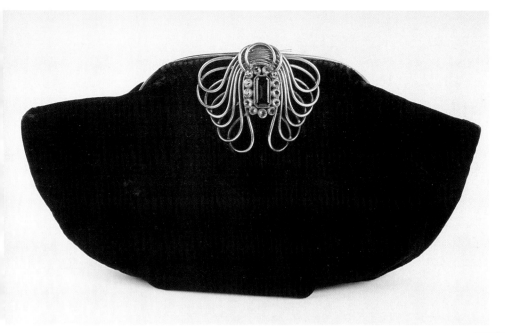

An art nouveau design on this clasp. 7.5" x 12".
Courtesy of Francine Cohen.

Marcasites on a sterling frame. 6" x 8.5". *Courtesy of Francine Cohen.*

Beautiful plique-à-jour bag with impressed design in fabric. 6.5" x 4". *Courtesy of Francine Cohen.*

White beaded bag with clear and green crystals on the frame. 7" x 7.5". *Courtesy of Francine Cohen.*

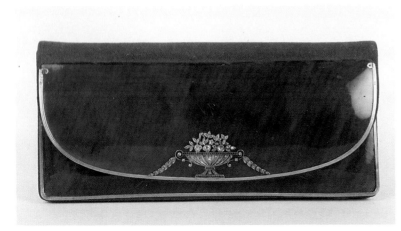

A very fine quality tortoiseshell bag with leather backing, decorated with rose diamonds, emeralds and gold trim. 3.75" x 7.5". *Courtesy of Francine Cohen.*

Tapestry body with a sterling frame decorated with torquoise and moonstones. "Made especially for Delman in France." 5.25" x 6.5". *Courtesy of Francine Cohen.*

Colored mesh bag by Whiting and Davis, Company. The frame is enamel on a gold-plated frame all in the original box. 7.5" x 5". *Courtesy of Francine Cohen.*

Sterling clip with inset scene of mother-of-pearl and Bakelite. Made in France for Sax-Kay of Detroit. 5.75" x 7". *Courtesy of Francine Cohen.*

Bakelite bag with an Oriental motif, and mirror inside. 6" x 4". *Courtesy of Francine Cohen.*

Enamel and marcasites on sterling buttons. Made in France exclusively for Bergdorf Goodman. 6.5" x 9". *Courtesy of Francine Cohen.*

Beautiful fine quality bag embroidered with gold thread and pearls, with a crystal and marcasite clasp. Made in France. 5" x 6". *Courtesy of Francine Cohen.*

Lizard skin bag trimmed in 14k gold. Decorated with a pull-out J.E. Caldwell & Company watch. Inside, the bag contains the original compact and lipstick. Marked, "E.F.R." 5.25" x 8". *Courtesy of Francine Cohen.*

Marblized Bakelite bag lined inside with leather, and decorated with a floral jade piece on the front. *Courtesy of Francine Cohen.*

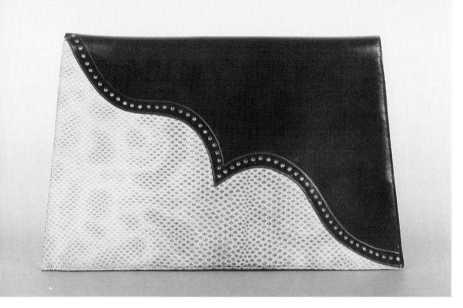

Leather and reptile skin bag made by I. Miller Beautiful Bags. 6'' x 9.5''. *Courtesy of Francine Cohen.*

German silver frame on this Deco purse, with a floral motif and two egrets on the back. 6'' x 9''. *Courtesy of Francine Cohen.*

Various glass stones and beads decorate this bag with a gold-plated frame. 6'' x 6.5''. *Courtesy of Francine Cohen.*

Rhinestones on base metal mesh bag. 6.5" x 6".
Courtesy of Francine Cohen.

Paste, chrysoprase and marcasite on sterling. 8" x 7". *Courtesy of Francine Cohen.*

Green and black enamel on sterling with acorn clasps. 8" x 6.5". *Courtesy of Francine Cohen.*

Opposite page: Two minaudières. One of green Bakelite with a silk tassel, and the other with sterling and marcasites on a faux tortoise shell, also with a silk tassel. Bodies measure 3" x 2.5". *Courtesy of Francine Cohen.*

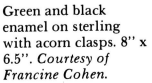

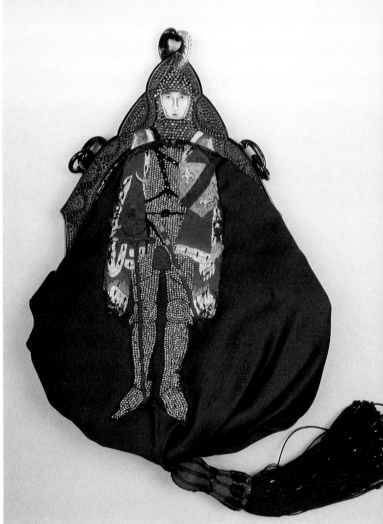

Gold colored metal frame on a purple tapestry, possibly from the Empire Period or Empire Revival. Maker unknown; marked déposé, made in France. 7" x 7.5". *Courtesy of Francine Cohen.*

A lady and her knight on either side! Bakelite faces and frames with beaded bodies and a silk tassel. Made in France. 9" x 6.25". *Courtesy of Francine Cohen.*

Fabulous red Bakelite accents with red beads. 6'' x 5.75''. *Courtesy of Francine Cohen.*

Victorian-styled Bakelite minaudière with carved rose and flower motif and silk tassel. Made in France. 6'' x 3.75''. *Courtesy of Francine Cohen.*

Black and white enamel on metal, Whiting and Davis Company. 5.5'' x 6''. *Courtesy of Francine Cohen.*

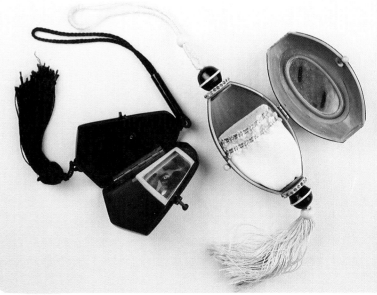

Two wonderful purses with tassels. *Courtesy of Bess Goodman.*

Green enamel and sterling over leather with a silk tassel. Deco. 5'' x 4.5''. *Courtesy of Francine Cohen.*

Metal and royal blue beads with silver frame. 6'' x 6.5''. *Courtesy of Kaylee Freedman.*

Black enamel and crushed egg shell with marcasites decorate this sterling frame on a sterling metal mesh body, 1920s. Also a black onyx clasp. Marked, Birks. 6.5'' x 5''. *Courtesy of Francine Cohen.*

Probably a homemade "kit" for a beaded bag, with plastic closure. 9'' x 7.5''. *Courtesy of Kaylee Freedman.*

Sterling silver frame with black beaded peacock design. 8'' x 10''. *Courtesy of Kaylee Freedman.*

German silver with metal and beaded body in a pouch style, accordion closure. 4.75'' x 8.75''. *Courtesy of Kaylee Freedman.*

Multi-colored glass beaded bag marked Ada Grunfeld, Austria. 8.75'' x 7.5''. *Courtesy of Kaylee Freedman.*

Deco-looking metal beaded bag. 6.5'' x 8.75''. *Courtesy of Kaylee Freedman.*

Metal frame with interesting beaded detail on the metal mesh body. 7'' x 8.75''. *Courtesy of Kaylee Freedman.*

A plastic frame and link chain with a beautiful beaded pattern. 6.5'' x 9.5''. *Courtesy of Kaylee Freedman.*

Metal frame with floral beaded pattern on the body. 7.25'' x 8.5''. *Courtesy of Kaylee Freedman.*

Sterling silver frame with clear beads and knitted body. 10'' x 8.5''. *Courtesy of Kaylee Freedman.*

A very Deco design on the frame and the body of this beaded bag. 10.5'' x 5.75''. *Courtesy of Kaylee Freedman.*

29

Bronze beads on a knitted body. 12" x 4.75".
Courtesy of Kaylee Freedman.

Beautiful beaded bag portraying a peacock. Same
design is displayed on the back. 6.75" x 15".
Courtesy of Mim Klein.

Pouch style bag with green stones and marcasites
on sterling. Marked Edwards Bags, Ltd. 7" x 3.5".
Courtesy of Kaylee Freedman.

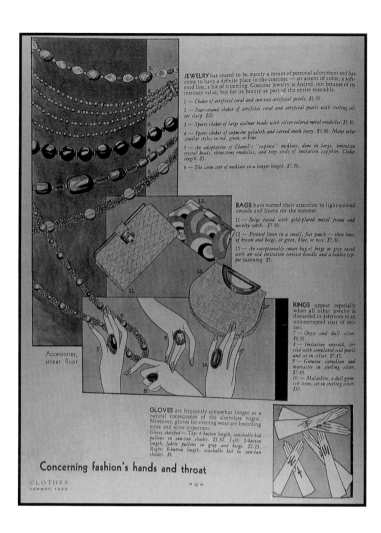

Black velvet (all original) with silver cupids. 9" w. x 7.5" l. *Courtesy of Mim Klein.*

Beaded handbag with cameo. Tagged, "Hervé Paris." Handmade in France. 8" x 6". *Courtesy of Mim Klein.*

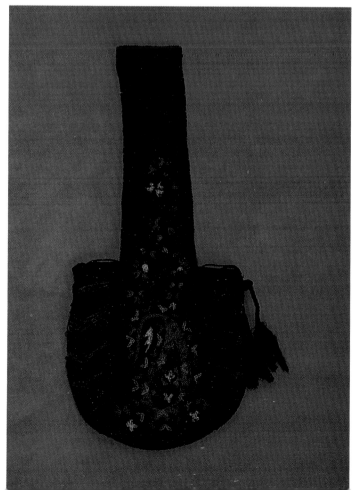

Victorian pull string bag in a pouch style. 14.5" x 7". *Courtesy of Kaylee Freedman.*

Victorian-style, beaded pouch bags. Probably
homemade kits. Each 5'' x 6''. *Courtesy of Kaylee
Freedman.*

Chapter 2

1930s—Deco to Depression

In the Depression era, those who were worst off were little concerned with fashion. Squalid "Hooverville" homes built of cardboard and corrugated iron scraps dotted the landscape, while the Salvation Army, Shirley Temple movies and Franklin Delano Roosevelt's New Deal tried desperately to quell the choruses of "Brother Can You Spare a Dime." Even for those more fortunate, those who could afford to be concerned with the *style* of their clothing and not just its warmth, things had changed.

The self-indulgent luxury of the '20s was over. In this time of hardship, handbag designers were forced to use less expensive metals in place of the 1920s' silver and gold for mesh and for handbag hardware. Imitation skins became very popular as well, and plastics such as Bakelite were carried over from other industries into handbag manufacturing. The scarcity of luxury materials, however, did not mean that manufacturers were frugal with their design talents. Indeed, the new forced reliance on artificial materials opened whole

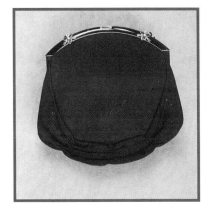

Black suede and enamel frame with marcasite bows. Rosenfeld Original. *Courtesy of Kaylee Freedman.*

Black suede bag with beaded decoration. *Courtesy of Kaylee Freedman.*

Black suede back with decorative clasp. *Courtesy of Kaylee Freedman.*

new vistas of fashion possibilities, and prompted great ingenuity. Resourceful big-name department stores often featured their own lines of handbags, mass-produced and inexpensive versions of the imaginative designer bags.

A few of the more cheerful 1930s trends included the new attention paid to coordinating accesories, the return of hand-tooled leather, and the continued popularity of enameled mesh bags. The famous Schiaparelli fashion line began with a series of whimsical, clever novelty bags. "Pochette" bags —envelope-style bags now commonly known as "clutches" —became popular as well, and pleats, piping and smocking were used to ornament cloth bags. The "slide fastener," more familiar to modern women as the "zipper," also made its first handbag appearance.

Brown suede bag with marcasite decorating the frame. 9.5" x 5.75". *Courtesy of Kaylee Freedman.*

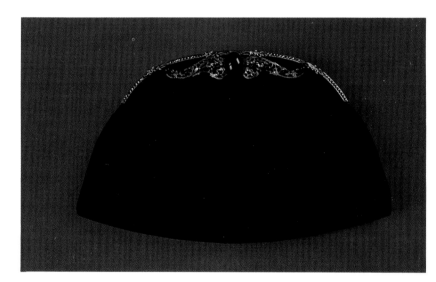

Black suede bag with silver metalwork. *Courtesy of Kaylee Freedman.*

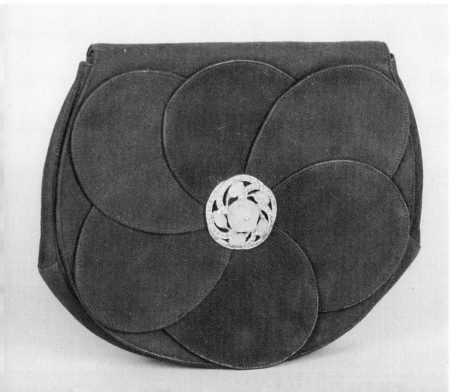

Mark Cross brown suede clutch with glass and rhinestone floral medallion, c. 1930s. 8" long. *Courtesy of Steppin' Out.*

A carnelian clasp with marcasites on sterling. 5.25" x 9.5". *Courtesy of Francine Cohen.*

Petit point bag made in Austria with decorative frame. 7.5" x 5.75". *Courtesy of Kaylee Freedman.*

Silk handbag with a yellow plastic clasp marked, "Made in England." *Courtesy of Cobra and Bellamy.*

Deco purse with enamel design on the sterling frame. 6.25" x 7". *Courtesy of Francine Cohen.*

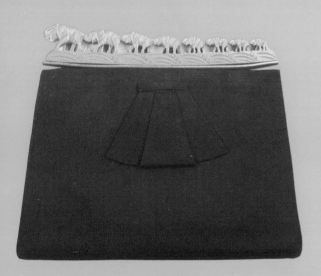

Black suede handbag with a pink plastic clasp, graduated elephants and a change purse inside. *Courtesy of Cobra and Bellamy.*

Pouch bag with ivory-like Bakelite frame. 7.5" x 7.5". *Courtesy of Francine Cohen.*

Leather purse with locusts, possibly from the Deco era. 5" x 8.5". *Courtesy of Francine Cohen.*

Green silk bag with a plastic handle of a yellow fox. A change purse is mounted inside. *Courtesy of Cobra and Bellamy.*

Deco purse with Bakelite on a sterling frame. 6.25" x 9.5". *Courtesy of Francine Cohen.*

Bakelite frame on sterling. 5.5" x 9.5". *Courtesy of Francine Cohen.*

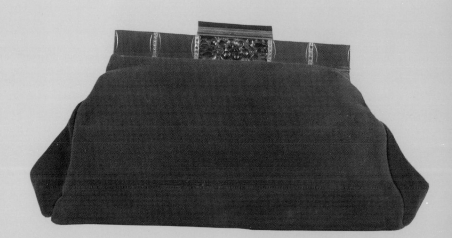

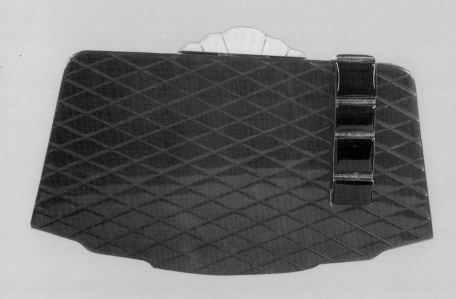

Bakelite Deco purse. "NRA Code Manufactured Under Ladies Handbag Code Authority." 6.25" x 9.75". *Courtesy of Francine Cohen.*

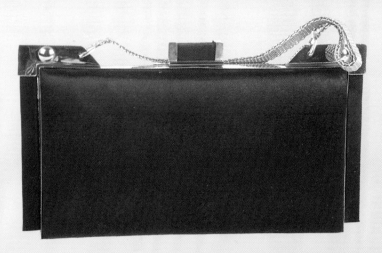

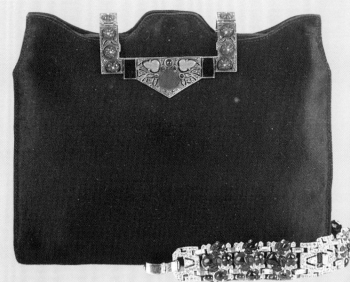

Interesting Art Deco purse with gold trim. Made by Industria Argentina, Argentina. 5" x 8.75". *Courtesy of Francine Cohen.*

Marcasites and various stones on sterling, often referred to as "fruit salad." 6" x 7.5". *Courtesy of Francine Cohen.*

A gold metal casing decorates this very Deco-looking purse. 5" x 8.75". *Courtesy of Francine Cohen.*

Deco style leather bag from the 1930s. Divided suede interior, signed Tarsis of Persia. Handle is a replacement. 12.5" x 8.5". *Courtesy of Peggy Ann Osborne.*

Needlepoint handbag, 1930s. 9'' x 11''. *Courtesy of Classics Illustrated, William Goldberg.*

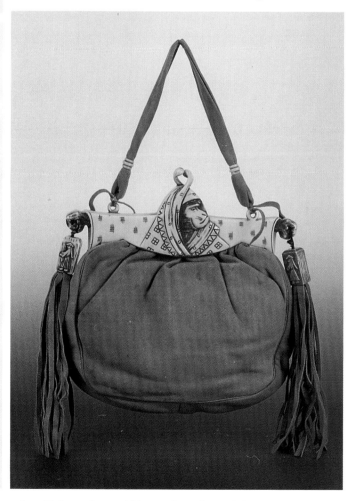

Art Deco purse with the Oriental motif of a fan, with gold trim and velvet. Made by Mondaine. 10.5'' x 12.25''. *Courtesy of Francine Cohen.*

An Oriental motif is sculpted on this Bakelite frame with a monkey and Oriental figures. 8.75'' x 9''. *Courtesy of Francine Cohen.*

Art Deco reticule with a green Bakelite top and steel colored beads. 8" x 4". *Courtesy of Francine Cohen.*

"The Normandie," from the 1930s, has a sterling frame, leather body and chrome smokestacks. Marked, "Déposé G.T." 6.25" x 10.75". *Courtesy of Francine Cohen.*

An interesting bead design decorates this Deco bag. 7.25" x 9". *Courtesy of Francine Cohen.*

Chalcedony, black onyx and marcasites decorate this Art Deco frame. 7" x 6.75". *Courtesy of Francine Cohen.*

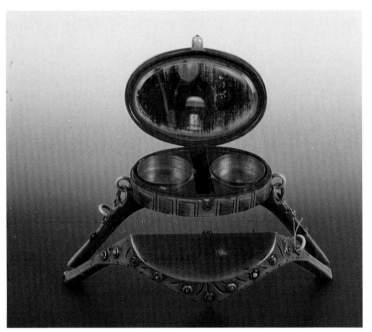

Bakelite frame opening two ways, from the 1930s.
The top hinges to reveal a compact and the front
opens to the purse itself. 2.5''-4.5'' x 7''. *Courtesy
of Francine Cohen.*

Beaded Deco purse, unmarked. 6.25'' x 9''.
Courtesy of Francine Cohen.

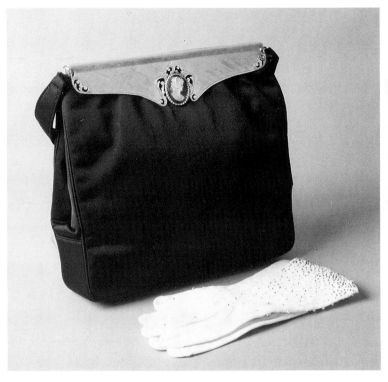

Black satin bag with cameo decoration on the frame. *Courtesy of Barbara Dollaway Michie.*

Gold metal bag with a mother-of-pearl decoration, 1920s-30s. Maker unknown. *Courtesy of Susann Spilkin.*

Beaded bag from the 1930s or 1940s. Bonwit Teller, Philadelphia. Made in France. 9.25'' x 6.25''. *Courtesy of Mim Klein.*

Unusual Bakelite decoration on this bag. 6.5'' x 9''.
Courtesy of Francine Cohen.

Art Deco cloth bag. Maybe American. 6''
w. x 5.5'' l. *Coutesy of Mim Klein.*

Art Deco purse with Bakelite on sterling
frame and a felt body. 6.5'' x 9''. *Courtesy
of Francine Cohen.*

Chapter 3

1940s—Sensible Styles for the Workplace

America was on top during the 1940s as prosperity and self-confidence returned. Patriotism ran high as the nation began an era of progress and leadership in all fields, from science and technology to fashion and the arts. American livng was revolutionized by the nation's efforts in preparation for World War II, by the years of military involvement, and at long last by the aftermath of the war. Women who had joined the fight overseas and those who had kept the country running at home found (and sometimes demanded to keep) their new roles in society and in the workplace.

Fashion followed this new female assertiveness, even in the field of handbag design. The soft, feminine beaded bags of the past were transformed almost by demand into large, boxy bags like those made by Fre-Mor. These bags were better matches for the sharp, broad-shouldered suit-dresses of the '40s and for the active lives of the responsible women who wore them.

Black beaded bag given by Philadelphia philanthropist Walter Annenburg, late 1930s-40s. *Courtesy of Barbara Dollaway Michie.*

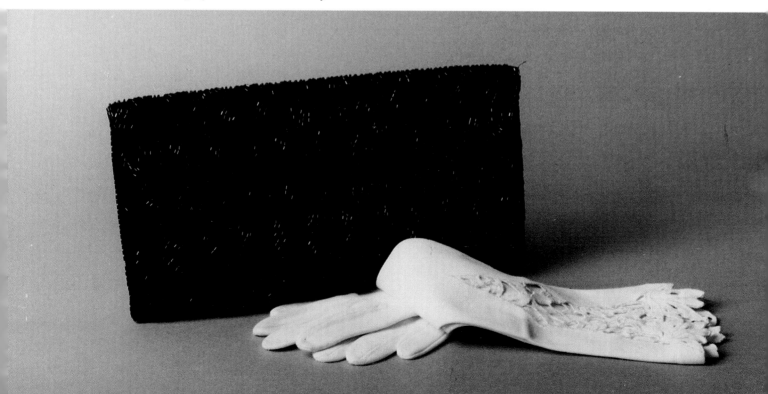

Animal skin bags were also the pre-and post-war craze. Exotic bags made of alligator, crocodile, turtle, lizard, or even walrus skin could turn any smart outfit into high fashion. Some collectors view bags displaying the claws or heads of the animals as "tourist trade" items with low appeal for handbag for handbag enthusiasts. Others either seek out or try to avoid whip-stitching on handbags. Whatever your personal preference, there are many bags from the 1940s still to be found.

Brown suede and gold lamé bag, 1940s. 4" x 6". *Courtesy of Classics Illustrated, William Goldberg.*

Black bag with ornate handle, c. 1945. *Courtesy of Margaret M. Nutt.*

Green Bakelite purse, early-1940s. *Courtesy of Wendy Tyson.*

Elegant black bag with change purse, c. 1945. Made by Lewis. *Courtesy of Margaret M. Nutt.*

A green leather bag, maker unknown, c. 1940s. 7''
x 7''. *Courtesy of Classics Illustrated, William
Goldberg*.

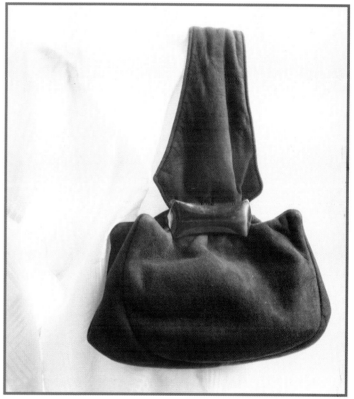

Pouch bag of brown suede. *Courtesy
of Piacente*.

Leather bag with tortoise shell frame by Ingberg, 1940s. 8.5" h. *Courtesy of Classics Illustrated, William Goldberg.*

Long clutch in the 1940s style with a bowtie pin attached. *Courtesy of Classics Illustrated, William Goldberg.*

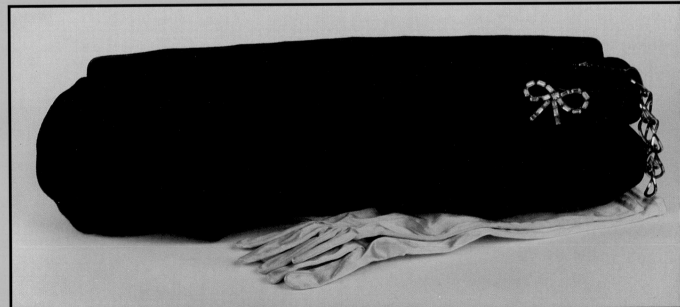

Brown felt bag with a Lucite clasp. Rosenfeld Original. 16" x 6". *Courtesy of Kaylee Freedman.*

Black calf bag with engraved brass plate marked "Le Denicheur." Right: signed inside, Rosenfeld, 6.25". Left: silver plate "Le Colin-Maillard." 11.5" x 11". *Courtesy of Rover and Lorber*

49

Three black suede and gold wire trim bags. Left to right: low drum shape with gold chain festoon, compact on lid. Made in France by Brevete. 3.75''; rectangular accordian bag with match case in one end and compact in the other end, also by Brevete. 5.5''; tall drum shape with compact lipstick and matches in one end. *Courtesy of Rover and Lorber*

Marcasite bag made in France for Harrods, 5.5'' x 8.5''.

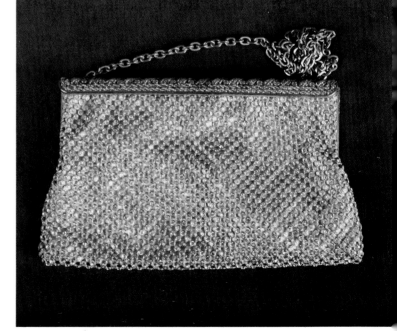

Gold finished leather handbag with gold lamé ruffle at the frame and as a single strap handle, 7.5" x 5". *Courtesy of Piacente*

Black satin handbag painted in polychrome glass beads with floral decoration, marked "Waldybag, Hand Painted, Made in England," 9" x 6". *Courtesy of Piacente*

Detailed cloth bag with gold trim, lid 5" x 7.25".

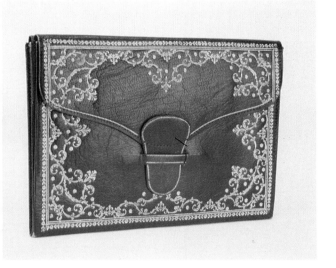

French tooled leather clutch with three openings on the top. 6" x 8.5". *Courtesy of Katy Kane*

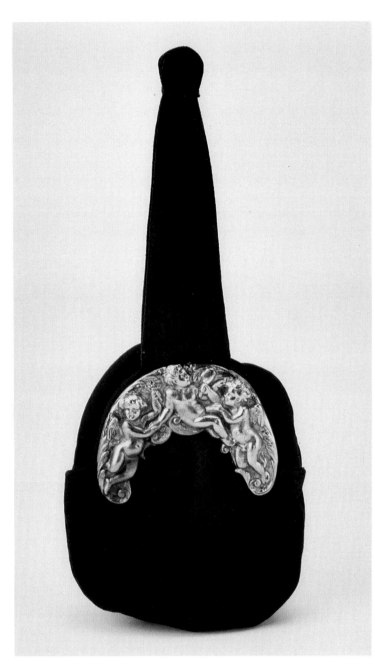

Brown cloth bag with metal frame of cupid decoration. 9" x 7.5". *Courtesy of Katy Kane.*

Lavendar Liberty & Co. of London bag with tassles. 9.5" x 10". *Courtesy of Katy Kane.*

Black kid bag with rectangular base and tapering sides, covered spring-hinged closure and two strap handles, 11.25'' x 7''. *Courtesy of Piacente*

Black wool bag with oval flat base, brass stud decorations, spring-hinged frame and single strap handle, 10'' x 6''. *Courtesy of Piacente*

Black French embroidered silk bag with beadwork on the frame. 8.5'' x 10.5''. *Courtesy of Katy Kane.*

Chain mail shoulder bag of gold and silver links with silver-finished leather lining. Marked "Raoul Calabro, Milano, New York," 9" x 6". *Courtesy of Piacente*

Black suede handbag with two brown plastic ring handles and interior zippered and open compartments, marked Lewis, 11.5" x 13". at handles. *Courtesy of Piacente*

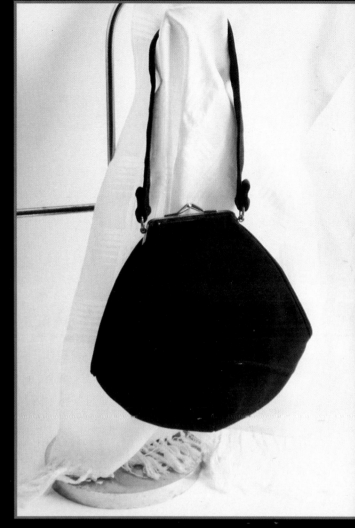

Blue suede bag of rounded and tapering shape with brass frame and clasp and single strap handle, marked "Coblentz Original," 8" x 8.5". *Courtesy of Piacente*

Black suede clutch/ handbag with folding snap closure, 10.5" x 4.25". *Courtesy of Piacente*

Brown cordé bag in swivelling brown plastic frame. Marked "Genuine Cordé." 9.75" x 8.5". *Courtesy of Steppin' Out.*

Group of three pony-skin handbags, all unmarked. Rectangular bag, 12" w. x 7.5" h. *Courtesy of Steppin' Out.*

Two bags with brown plastic expandable frames. Left: dark blue beaded bag with three compartments by DuBonnette. Right: brown calf with three separate compartments. 10.25" x 4.5". *Courtesy of Steppin' Out.*

Two Mexican bags with double opening frames. Left: red calf marked "Originales Artel." 8.75" x 8". Right: pony skin marked Olvera. 7" x 7". *Courtesy of Steppin' Out.*

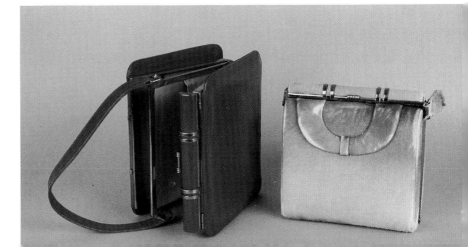

Three handbags of similar design with folding handles. Made of blue kid leather, red kid leather and black wool, marked Debbie Jerome. *Courtesy of Steppin' Out.*

Red kid bag with a folding closure and brass clasp, chain (may be a restoration) and a strap handle, 8.5'' x 7.5''. *Courtesy of Piacente*

Red kid clutch bag with suede interior and folding closure with sliding tongue clasp, 14'' x 7.75''. *Courtesy of Piacente*

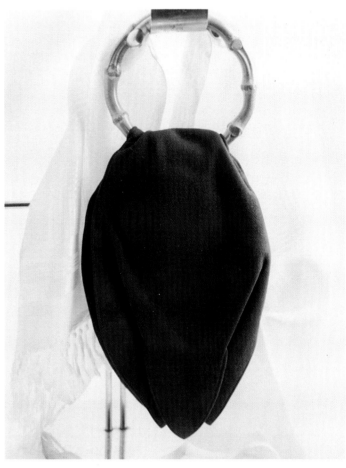

Brown suede bag with coiled bamboo handle and long, leaf-shaped flap with round, brass bound closure and interior pockets. Marked "B. Altman & Co., Paris and New York, Made in France," 12". *Courtesy of Piacente*

Black wool bag marked "Lewis" with single strap handle and interior gold finished mirror and comb, key case and change purse, 10" x 8". *Courtesy of Piacente*

Multicolored plastic sections are connected with plastic thread, 1940s. 6.25" x 11". *Courtesy of Katy Kane.*

Silver leather handbag marked "Naitan, Hecho en Mexico." Brass catch. 10.75" x 10.5". *Courtesy of Steppin' Out*

Blue calf clutch with white piping trim and enameled blue and white metal decoration. 7.75" x 6". *Courtesy of Steppin' Out.*

Three 1940s clutch bags. Left: brown and white plastic tile purse, 11.5" x 7.25". Right: brown and white tile with hand snaps and looped handle. Center: colorful tile designed by Jorve. *Courtesy of Steppin' Out.*

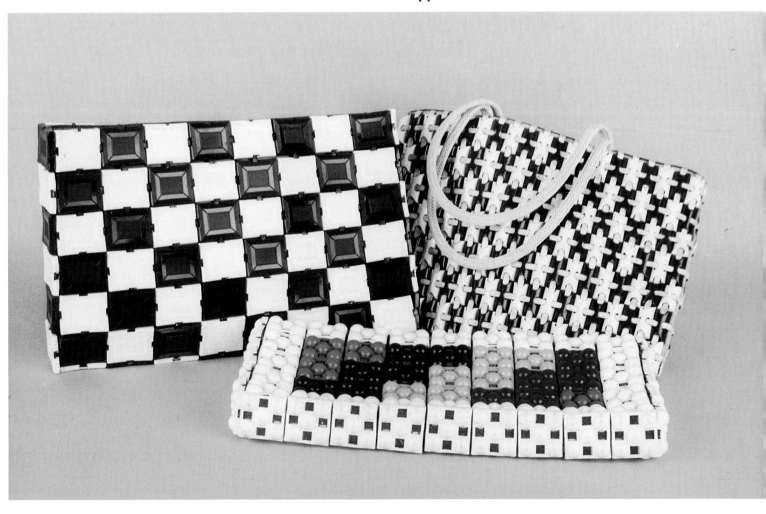

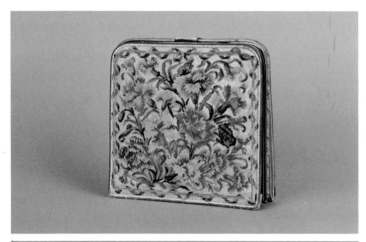

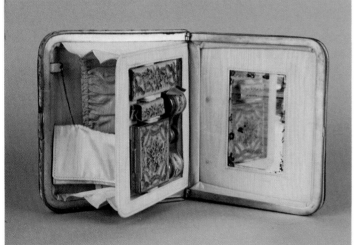

Petit point over grained gold leather fitted with mirror, opera glasses, comb, lipstick slide and compact, and change purse. 6.5'' x 6'' h. *Courtesy of Steppin' Out.*

Two red leather handbags. In back; 1940s clutch with twisted brass bracelet handle signed Ovington's, Fifth Avenue, New York. In front; roll bag with two straps and brass catch. 10.5'' x 4''. *Courtesy of Steppin' Out.*

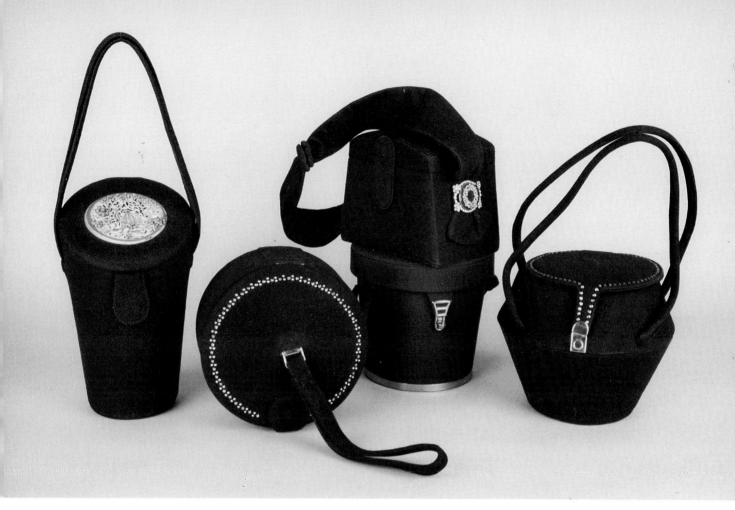

Group of 1940s box bags, left to right: black cashmere with slanted lid and beaded medallion. 8.25'' h.; black suede, round, with rhinestone trim by Surrey Original. 4'' h.; black suede with two paste and enamel side decorations. Rosenfeld Original. 5.5'' x 5''; dark blue round tapered box, Navy Faille; black suede trapezoid round shape with rhinestone trim, 6'' h. *Courtesy of Steppin' Out.*

Red box-style alligator bag with ship-like bottom. 9'' x 4.5''. *Courtesy of Kaylee Freedman.*

Beautiful red Argentina alligator. 9.5'' x 9.5''. *Courtesy of Kaylee Freedman.*

Box-style alligator bag with Bakelite strap and mirror inside. 8.5" x 4.25". *Courtesy of Kaylee Freedman.*

This unusual triangular shaped Argentinian alligator bag has three compartments, one for cigarettes, one for paper and one for powder. 3.25" x 4.75". *Courtesy of Kaylee Freedman.*

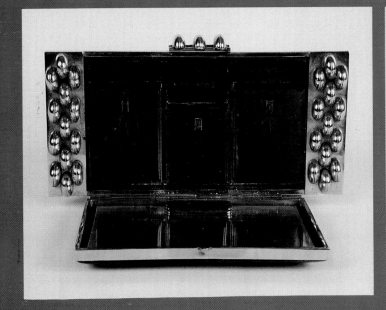

Unusual alligator clutch with brass detail. Open shot shows three compartments and a mirror. 9.25" x 4.5". *Courtesy of Kaylee Freedman.*

Unusual alligator "bubble" bag marked, "Madeline Bag." 9" x 6.5". *Courtesy of Kaylee Freedman.*

Black Argentina alligator bag. Interesting shape, 4" x 6". *Courtesy of Kaylee Freedman.*

Black box alligator bag made by Sterling, USA. 7" x 5.5". *Courtesy of Kaylee Freedman.*

Bell shaped green alligator bag. 8.75" x 8.5". *Courtesy of Kaylee Freedman.*

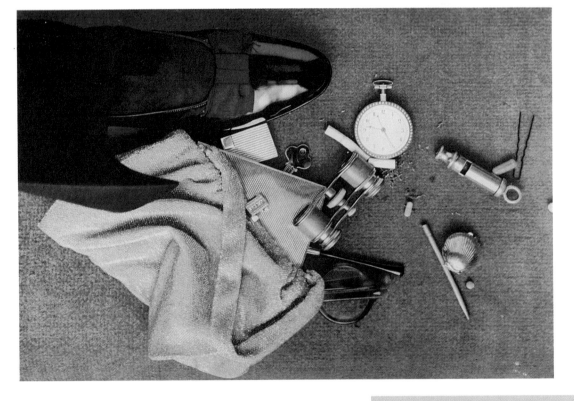

Honey-colored alligator bag with an interesting
frazzled clasp. 10.5'' x 7.5''. *Courtesy of Kaylee
Freedman.*

Camera-case style alligator bag. 9'' x 9''. *Courtesy
of Kaylee Freedman.*

Honey-colored whipstitched bag with double compartments. 8.5" x 6.2". *Courtesy of Kaylee Freedman.*

Above and left:
Unusual "wave"-style bag with a side closure and mirror on lid. 8.5" x 6.5". *Courtesy of Kaylee Freedman.*

Box bag of Industria Argentina camen crocodile. The bag has a key lock. 9.5" x 6.5". *Courtesy of Kaylee Freedman.*

Barrel-shaped bag with pedestal base made of green snake skin. Berger Handbags, New York. 8" x 7". *Courtesy of Kaylee Freedman.*

Hatbox-style, honey-colored alligator bag with Bakelite handle. 8.75" x 8". *Courtesy of Kaylee Freedman.*

Turtle skin envelope bag marked Gambini. 12.5" x 5.25". *Courtesy of Kaylee Freedman.*

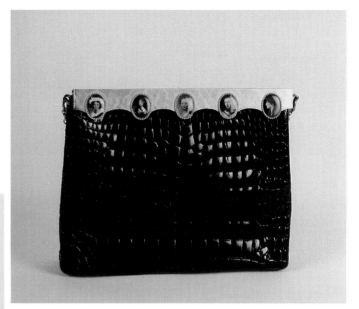

Black alligator marked "Cyreld, Paris" with cameos along the frame. 8.5" x 6.5". *Courtesy of Kaylee Freedman.*

Brown crocodile bag with silver trim. 9" x 7". *Courtesy of Kaylee Freedman.*

Box style alligator bag with a Bakelite closure and a change purse. 9" x 6.5". *Courtesy of Kaylee Freedman.*

Three skin bags, from left to right: brown envelope-style crocodile bag from Argentina with silver tips, 11" x 6.5"; brown alligator clutch, 12" x 7" x 4"; Argentinian envelope-style clutch, 12" x 8". *Courtesy of Kaylee Freedman.*

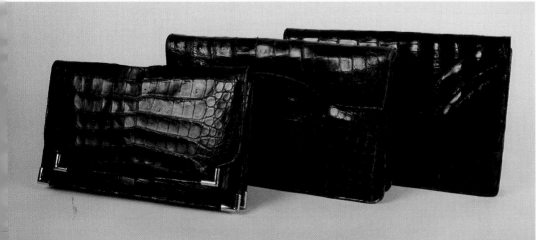

A bell-shaped chocolate brown crocodile bag. 8" x 7". *Courtesy of Kaylee Freedman.*

Elegant green alligator. 9.5" x 5.75". *Courtesy of Kaylee Freedman.*

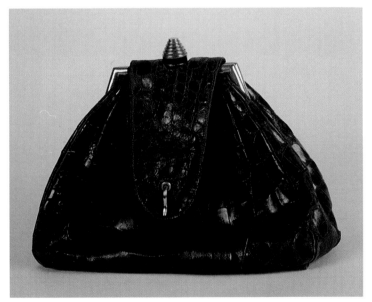

This alligator bag is of an unusual soft bell shape. 10" x 8". *Courtesy of Kaylee Freedman.*

Exquisite red alligator bag. 7.5" x 8". *Courtesy of Kaylee Freedman.*

Honey-colored Argentinian alligator. 9" x 5.5".
Courtesy of Kaylee Freedman.

Left: Deauville chocolate brown alligator bag with
a double strap; 6.5" x 8". Right: Argentinian
medium brown bag with clasps on either side; 8.5"
x 6.75". *Courtesy of Kaylee Freedman.*

Doctor's bag style, red alligator bag with an off
balance half sphere for a clasp. 11" x 6.75".
Courtesy of Kaylee Freedman.

The bag on the left is alligator, 13" x 9.5". On the right is an alligator bag made in France with fine leather lining the inside, 10.5" x 6.75". *Courtesy of Kaylee Freedman.*

Argentinian alligator, envelope-style bag. 9.5" x 6.5". *Courtesy of Kaylee Freedman.*

Black turtle-skin bag with double compartments. 8.5" x 5.75". *Courtesy of Kaylee Freedman.*

Chocolate brown alligator bag which opens to two pockets. 14.75'' x 7.5''. *Courtesy of Kaylee Freedman.*

Alligator bag with belt buckle style clasp. 8.5'' x 6.75''. *Courtesy of Kaylee Freedman.*

Brown alligator bag. 9.5'' x 8.75''. *Courtesy of Kaylee Freedman.*

Left: black box-style alligator bag, 8" x 7". Right: brown alligator, 9.5" x 6.75". *Courtesy of Kaylee Freedman.*

A wonderful, honey-colored alligator bag with silver lock and key closure. 7" x 4". *Courtesy of Kaylee Freedman.*

Honey-colored Argentinian alligator bag. 11" x 7.25". *Courtesy of Kaylee Freedman.*

This skin bag is interesting because it opens with side clasps. *Courtesy of Kaylee Freedman.*

Alligator bag with tapering sides, covered frame, and strap handle, marked "Deitsch," 13" x 8.5". *Courtesy of Piacente*

Alligator bag trimmed with gold metal and accessories to match. *Courtesy of Anne Hopkin.*

Beautiful red alligator bag. *Courtesy of Kaylee Freedman.*

Brown alligator with unique metal clasp. 10.75" x 7.25". *Courtesy of Kaylee Freedman.*

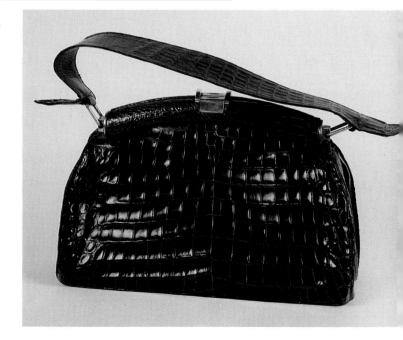

Brown alligator bag with wide handle. 7.75" x 7.5". *Courtesy of Kaylee Freedman.*

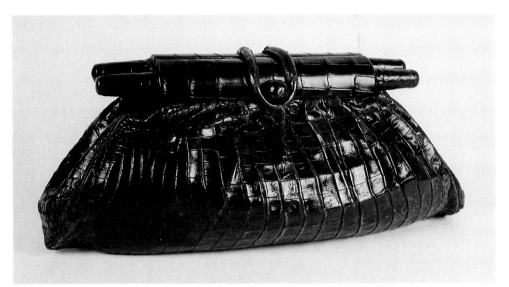

Pouch-style alligator clutch. 14"
x 8.5". *Courtesy of Kaylee
Freedman.*

Honey-colored alligator bag from Argentinian
alligator. 13" x 8.75". *Courtesy of Kaylee
Freedman.*

Honey-colored clutch bag. 12" x 7". *Courtesy of
Kaylee Freedman.*

This alligator bag with silver clasps opens to double compartments. 10" x 6.5". *Courtesy of Kaylee Freedman.*

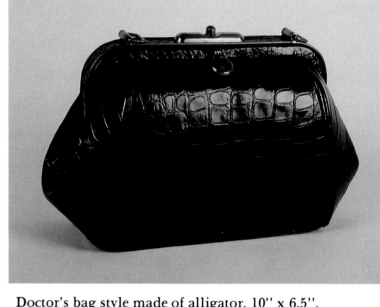

Doctor's bag style made of alligator. 10" x 6.5". *Courtesy of Kaylee Freedman.*

Honey-colored alligator bag made in Cuba. 9" x 7.5". *Courtesy of Kaylee Freedman.*

Green alligator bag. 8.5" x 7.5". *Courtesy of Kaylee Freedman.*

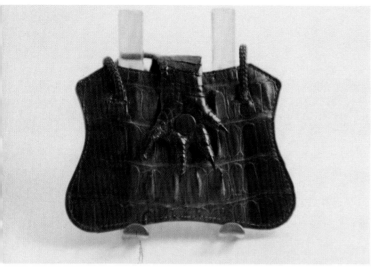

Alligator wallet with claw snap closure and a change purse and two pockets inside. Fitted with replacement long string handles. Originally with short leather handles. *Courtesy of Piacente*

Rectangular alligator bag with brass catch and single strap handle marked "Made in France for Coblentz," 9" x 6". *Courtesy of Piacente*

Triangular alligator bag with original strap handle, 10" x 6". *Courtesy of Piacente*

Alligator bag with plastic frame and replaced handle, original handle was similar woven leather, 10.75" x 8". *Courtesy of Piacente*

Green alligator clutch bag in hard frame with brass rim and hinged clasp, 8". x 4". *Courtesy of Piacente*

Small alligator bag with an interesting shape, probably American, with zippered closure, 9". x 7". *Courtesy of Piacente*

Advertising sign of a scrolled sign, "Alligator makes sense," 15.25" x 13.25". *Courtesy of Piacente*

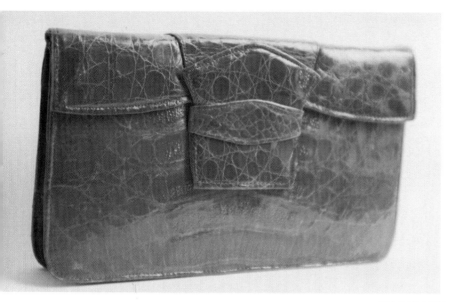

Alligator clutch with envelope flap, circa 1944, with leather lining marked "Industria Argentina, Made in Argentine, Genuine Alligator," 11.75" x 6.5". *Courtesy of Piacente*

Red alligator shoulder bag with folding closure and brass turning clasp, marked "Lucille de Paris, Genuine Alligator, Made in USA," 10" x 9.5". *Courtesy of Piacente*

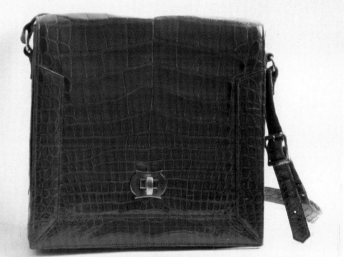

Black faux alligator cosmetic case by Harriet Hubbard Ayer fitted with bottles and containers in a special compartment which folds out of one side, 18" x 11.5". *Courtesy of Piacente*

Suitcase of highly textured alligator skin, 16'' x 11.5''. *Courtesy of Piacente*

Black alligator handbag with two strap handles and brass frame with clasp, rectangular bottom on four brass feet and tapering folded sides, 14.5'' x 9.25''. *Courtesy of Piacente*

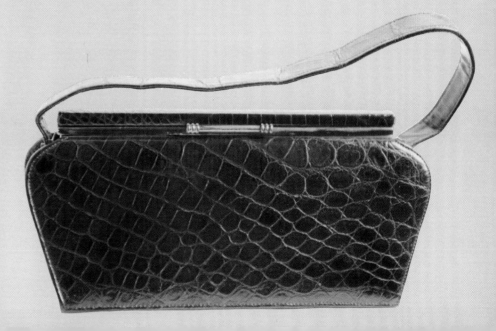

Alligator purse with flat bottom and long sides joined by a brass bar clasp and single strap handle, 11.25'' x 5''. *Courtesy of Piacente*

Red crocodile clutch bag with a brass frame and clasp and leather lining, 12'' x 6''. *Courtesy of Piacente*

Brown alligator bag in beautiful condition with a folding closure and two brass catches, marked "Made in France expressly for Alexander's," 8.5'' x 6''. *Courtesy of Piacente*

Alligator clutch bag labeled "Bag by Black," with brown plastic catch, 14.5'' x 7''. *Courtesy of Piacente*

Long alligator wallet with claw snap closure and an interior change purse and two pockets, 6.25'' x 3.5''. *Courtesy of Piacente*

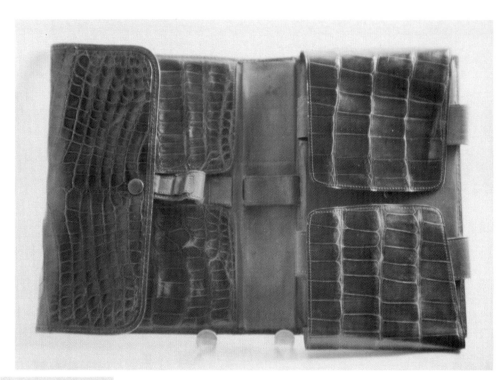

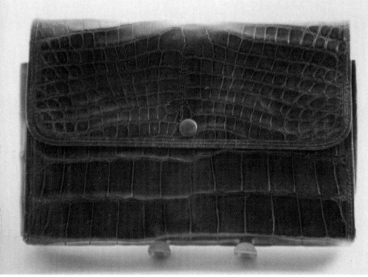

Alligator dressing kit with leather interior, containers missing. (shown open and closed). *Courtesy of Piacente*

Dark blue alligator handbag with flat bottom and gathered sides joined by a brass frame and catch, and double strap handles. *Courtesy of Piacente*

Alligator bag by Belle of New York with two strap handles, not an unusual shape but of particularly nice caramel colored leather and nicely made. 10" x 7". *Courtesy of Piacente*

Folding paper fan with alligator-covered end ribs 9". *Courtesy of Piacente*

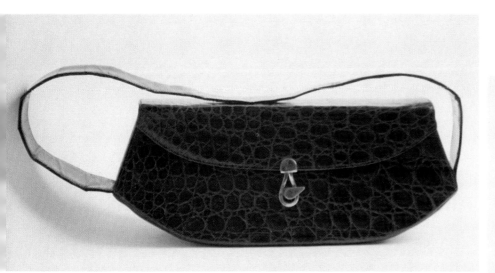

Rectangular alligator handbag with folding closure and brass clasp, single strap handle, 11.25" x4.5". *Courtesy of Piacente*

Black alligator bag with enamel work on frame marked "Moralito, Paris." 7" x 9". *Courtesy of Katy Kane.*

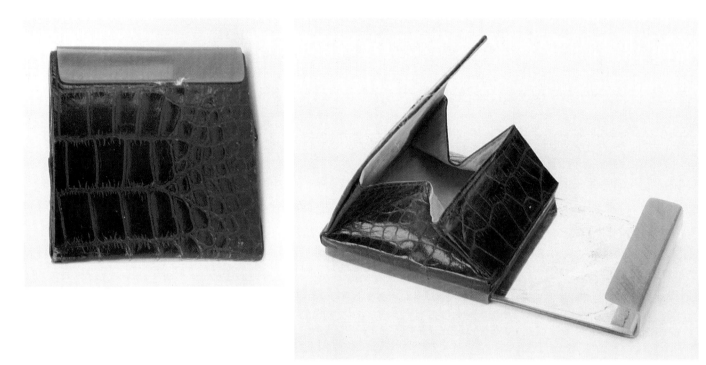

Black alligator and Bakelite mirror and powder compact. (Shown open and closed). 4'' x 4''. *Courtesy of Katy Kane.*

Two alligator bags. Left: baby alligator on flap and interior compartments, 10.5'' x 6.5''. Right: two oval flaps, marked "Made in Cuba." 9'' x 7.25''. *Courtesy of Steppin' Out.*

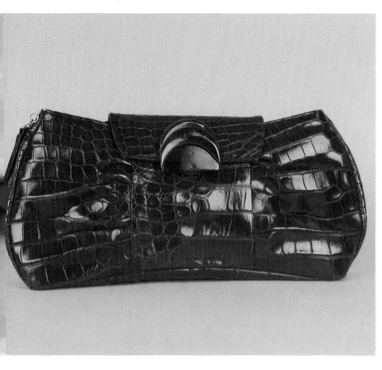

Brown alligator clutch with brown plastic catch. 15" x 7.5". *Courtesy of Steppin' Out.*

Dark brown alligator bag with missing handle. 9" x 7.5". *Courtesy of Kaylee Freedman.*

Honey-colored alligator bag, unmarked. 9.5" x 6.5". *Courtesy of Kaylee Freedman.*

Green alligator handbag with oval flat base and gathered sides with brass frame and side clasps and a single wide strap handle, 6.5" x 8". *Courtesy of Piacente*

Alligator pouch bag with brass catch and two strap handles. Unmarked. 11" x 6". *Courtesy of Piacente*

Red alligator bag with drawstring finish on one side, zipper closure and two open pockets, 11" x 8". *Courtesy of Piacente*

Brown pieced alligator clutch bag with envelope folded closure and plastic knife clasp, marked "Deitsch," 17" x 8.5". *Courtesy of Piacente*

Black alligator with brass catch and single handle. Marked "Edith Uffner" for Bonwit Teller. 12" x 7.25". *Courtesy of Piacente*

Two-tone alligator bag with actual alligator claws displayed on front of bag. Plastic frame. 9.25" x 6.5". *Courtesy of Piacente*

Small, brown, boat-shaped alligator bag. Unmarked. 11.5". *Courtesy of Piacente*

Tall black alligator bag with brass frame and single wristhandle. Two sides open to show a red leather interior. The worn tag may read "Elizabeth Arden." 5.25" x 6.5". *Courtesy of Piacente*

Black alligator envelope handbag with single strap handle and three brushed brass clasp pieces. This bag has a red leather interior and was made by Rosenfeld. Marked "Genuine Alligator." 11.5" x 7". *Courtesy of Piacente*

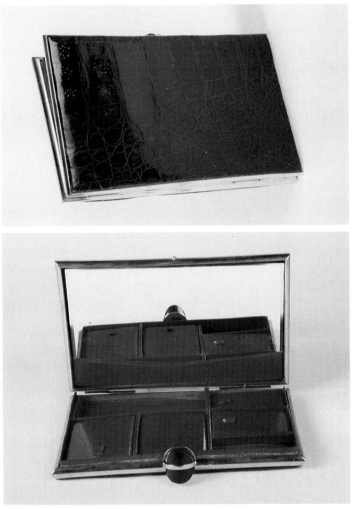

Brown alligator bag with single handle. Made in France by Coblentz. 9" x 6". *Courtesy of Piacente*

Alligator jewelry case. *Courtesy of Piacente.*

Two rectangular alligator bags. The left has a snap closure and single handle, unmarked. 9.5" x 4". The right is marked "by Alan" and has a mirror under the lid. 9" x 3". *Courtesy of Piacente*

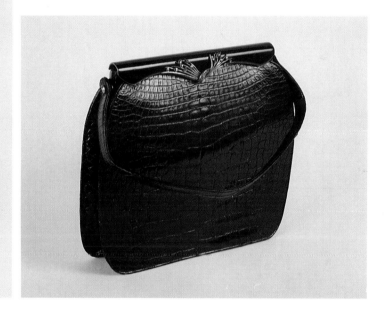

Large black alligator bag with single handle and top brass clasp. Marked "Dofan" made in France. *Courtesy of Piacente*

Red alligator handbag, c. 1940. Marked, "Jacqueline mode bag reg. in USA by David Stair." 8.5" x 7.75". *Courtesy of Katy Kane.*

Pin and earrings made of alligator and cloth. Pin, 7" long. *Courtesy of Piacente.*

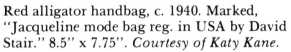

Elegant black alligator bag with a silver and rhinestone decoration on the frame. Rendl Original. *Courtesy of Susann Spilkin.*

Alligator clutch with a rectangular catch. Made by U. Bag Co. 12.5" x 7". *Courtesy of Piacente*

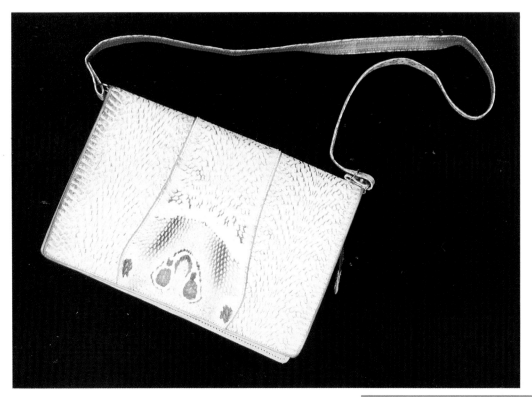

Double sided cobra skin with back pouch for cosmetics. 9.5" x 6.5". *Courtesy of Peggy Ann Osborne.*

White lizard handbag and clutch. The handbag is by Palizzio, New York. The clutch, with a silver and turquoise frame and clasp, is by Art Craft. 8" x 6". *Courtesy of Route 66 Antiques.*

Red alligator bag marked Deitsch. Label reads Milgrim. 8" x 9.5". *Courtesy of Route 66 Antiques.*

Black alligator bag with baby claw on the front
and a silver clasp. Also comes with matching
wallet, change purse and gloves. Signed Ledere
Courtesy of Susann Spilkin.

Pouch alligator bag with plastic frame. Label reads
"Wilshire." 12" x 7.5". *Courtesy of Piacente*

Walrus skin bag with the old lock system to close.
16" x 11.5". *Courtesy of Piacente*

Dark brown alligator bag with the alligator's head
and feet on the front. *Courtesy of Piacente*

Left: bell shaped bag, 8.5" x 7.5". Right: brown bag, 1950s, 10" x 9.5". *Courtesy of Kaylee Freedman.*

Brown suede and lizard bag with slightly tapering sides and folding closure with brass clasp and two strap handles, 6.75" sq. *Courtesy of Piacente*

"Kamra Pak" purse, c. 1940s. Metal body overlaid with lizard skin. A pocket on one side opens to a compact. It gives the appearance of opening like a camera. 5.25" x 3.25". *Courtesy of Francine Cohen.*

Two leather clutch bags: brown with envelope closing and two interior compartments, 12" x 8"; black "Genuine Buffalo" with snap flap closing and interior change purse and zipper compartment, 9.75" x 6.5". *Courtesy of Piacente*

Chapter 4

1950s—The New Look

In the '50s, finally free of economic or wartime worries, people could turn their attention to the pleasure and excitement of prosperity and progress. Public attention was divided between new stage shows like "West Side Story" and all the programs they could watch at home on their new color televisions. In this comfortable, even complacent atmosphere, Grace Kelly, Audrey Hepburn and Doris Day became famous, each with her own variation of the "1950s look" of ladylike elegance and self-possession.

Hermés created the "Kelly Bag" shape in 1892 with no idea that the bag would eventually take its place in twentieth century fashion as the epitome of this 1950s "ladylike" look. Hermés' bag, called a "sac haut à courroie" or "high-handle" bag, was originally much larger and more rugged, intended to be used for carrying saddles. Hermès craftsmen later scaled down the proportions to meet women's needs.

Metal and plastic handbag with clear plastic handle by Dorset-Rex, 1950s. 6" x 6". *Courtesy of Classics Illustrated, William Goldberg.*

Plastic handbag with 24k gold plated top, by Tyrolean, c. 1956. 3.5" x 6.25". *Courtesy of Classics Illustrated, William Goldberg.*

White plastic bag in the shape of a pail, by Rialto, of New York. *Courtesy of Bess Goodson.*

The beloved actress-turned-Princess Grace Kelly owned one of these bags. When she appeared on the cover of *Life* magazine carrying the handled Hermés bag, it was immediately christened the "Kelly bag". That bag and Princess Grace suited one another so well that the bag's popular name has never changed. Soon after this photograph appeared, almost every manufacturer began designing its own version of this classic status bag.

According to a 1951 article in *Handbags and Accessories*, the production of beaded bags remained a European art until World War II put many European luxury goods out of reach. With the haute couture of the Old World inaccessible, Americans were forced to use their own resources in making beaded bags; soon, American beaded bags took on a greater share of the home market.

Beaded bags became much more versatile, designed not just for evening wear but for day wear as well. Joseph Newman of Gold Seal Importers became one of the largest American producers of all types of hand-beaded bags. Under his label "Bags by Josef," he originated "caviar beading," which became a big day-wear hit among American women of the 1950s.

When plastic handbags came in vogue, they reflected the era's fetish for abstract and modern design, and allowed the whimsical side of the fifties to surface. Bags of Lucite and other plastics became the rage for women of all ages, from the rock-n-roll teeny bopper to the mature adult woman, and bags were manufactured for formal wear as well as for casual novelty use.

Two Lewsid Jewels by Llewellyn, 1950s. Each is plastic with metal frame and clasp, 8" x 7" x 5". *Courtesy of Susann Spilkin.*

Brown plastic bag with two levels, hinged marked, "Wilardy." *Courtesy of Bess Goodson.*

Grey bag with metal decoration and curved plastic clasp. Made by Wilardy Originals, 1950s. 3" x 7.5" x 4.5". *Courtesy of Dianne Rosenberg.*

Yellowish-ivory colored plastic bag with split handle, maker unknown. 6" x 7" x 3.5". *Courtesy of Dianne Rosenberg.*

Black plastic bag with rhinestones decorating the top. Unknown maker, 1950s. 9" x 4" x 3". *Courtesy of Susann Spilkin.*

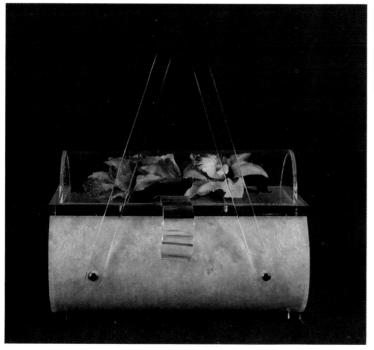

This plastic bag was often referred to as the "coffin" bag resembling a coffin laid out with flowers. Possibly by Harry Litwin. 5" x 7.5" x 4.75". *Courtesy of Dianne Rosenberg.*

Sleek, black plastic handbag with metal clasp, 1950s. 3.5'' x 9''. *Courtesy of Classics Illustrated, William Goldberg.*

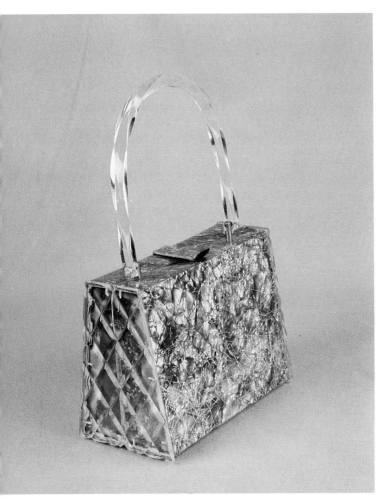

Grey plastic bag by ''Henryfrank Palm Springs, California.'' *Courtesy of Bess Goodson.*

Grey bag in soft half-circle shape, early 1950s. Lewsid Jewel by Llewellyn Inc. 8'' x 5.5''. *Courtesy of Radio Times.*

William Goldberg shows off his bags. Collectors go crazy looking for different and fun types of handbags.

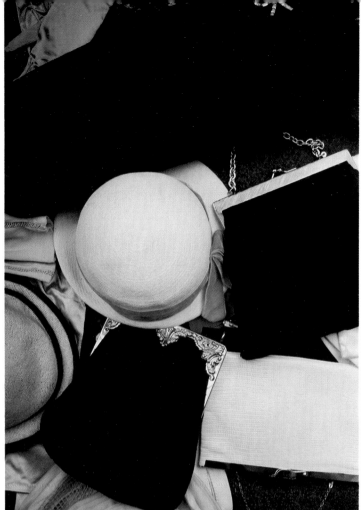

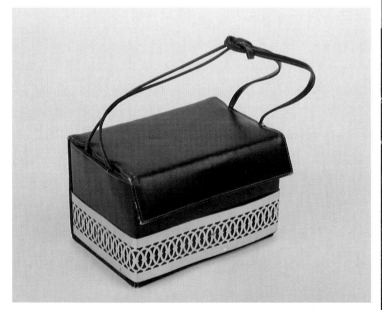

Leather box bag with metal decoration, 1950s. 4'' x 6.75''. *Courtesy of Classics Illustrated, William Goldberg.*

Collage of bags.

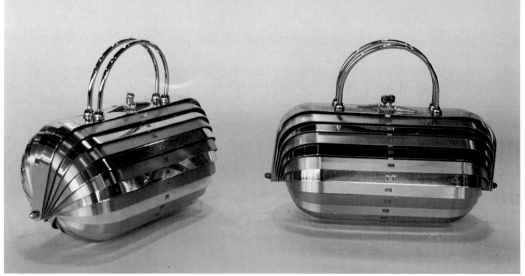

Two brushed aluminum handbags, one in silver, the other in gold tones. Oval slats make up the design. 9'' long. *Courtesy of Rover and Lorber*

Clear vinyl bag with velvety black flowers, 1950s. *Courtesy of Anne Hopkin.*

1950s straw handbag, maker unknown. *Courtesy of Classics Illustrated, William Goldberg.*

Clear vinyl bag with gold details and gold chain, 1950s. *Courtesy of Anne Hopkin.*

Emilio Pucci bag. *Courtesy of Kaylee Freedman.*

Vinyl and silver lace bag with silver frame. 5" x 7". *Courtesy of Peggy Ann Osborne.*

1950s vinyl horse and elephant purses. 6" h. *Courtesy of Rover and Lorber*

Black calf leather bag, maker unknown, c. 1950s.
2.75'' x 9''. *Courtesy of Classics Illustrated,
William Goldberg.*

A decorative felt turtle for this wicker bag, 1950s.
Signed Midas, Miami Beach. 8.5'' x 8''. *Courtesy of
Classics Illustrated, William Goldberg.*

White cultured pearl bag with pearl collar. Davids
imports Made in Japan. *Courtesy of Peggy Ann
Osborne.*

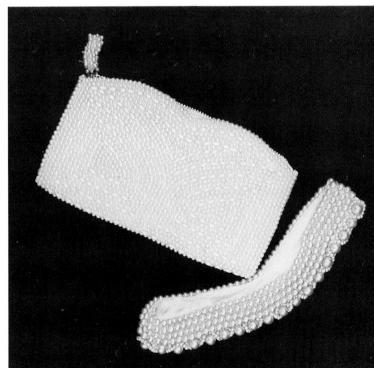

Gold lamé handbag with matching shoes, 1950s.
4'' x 8.5''. *Courtesy of Classics Illustrated, William
Goldberg.*

Gold leather clutch by Hattie Carnegie, Inc., 9'' x
5.25''. *Courtesy of Rover and Lorber*

Three metal baskets, left to right: large with two
top flaps. 9.25'' x 5.75''; medium size by Goldstrom
with drawstring closure. 8.5'' x 6''; smallest 6'' x
5.5''. *Courtesy of Steppin' Out.*

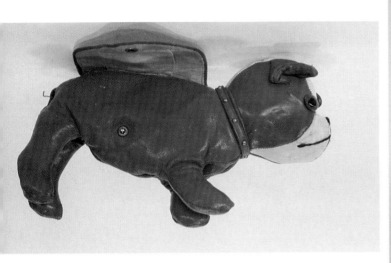

Adorable child's bulldog with snap side closing. 8.75" long. *Courtesy of Steppin' Out.*

This straw bag decorated with fruit was made in Spain. *Courtesy of Anne Hopkin.*

Accordian top bag. *Courtesy of Rover and Lorber, NYC*

Clutch marked Martin. *Courtesy of Anne Hopkin.*

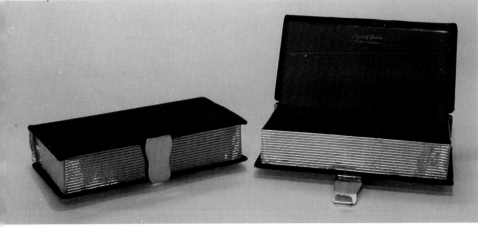

Two "book" design bags by Elizabeth Arden, one of blue faille and the other of brown suede. 7.5" long. *Courtesy of Steppin' Out.*

A leopard hand warmer that has a zipper for a handbag as well. *Courtesy of Anne Hopkin.*

Navy leather and ecru fabric "Kelly" bag marked "made in Italy for Coblentz." 10" x 13". *Courtesy of Katy Kane.*

Brown bag with amber clasp. *Courtesy of Anne Hopkin.*

Black French handbag decorated with bees on frame. 6.5" x 10". *Courtesy of Katy Kane.*

Fortuny bag. 12.5'' x 12''.
Courtesy of Katy Kane.

Left: black suede bag, 10'' x 3''.
Right: black satin bag by Garay, 8''.
Courtesy of Route 66 Antiques.

Tooled leather bags shown with
matching belt. Left: folding top with
tooled leaf design. 9'' x 7.25''. Center:
heart-shaped bag. Right: tooled
leather bag with pierced leaf design
on light background, marked
Davalos, Mexico. 10.75'' x 10.5''.
Courtesy of Steppin' Out.

A floral design decorates the lid of this ivory bag. *Courtesy of Anne Hopkin.*

Thick pile needle point tapestry with German buildings as motif, gold frame. Made in W. Germany. 9" x 9". *Courtesy of Peggy Ann Osborne.*

A leopard skin bag with accessories to match. *Courtesy of Anne Hopkin.*

Enjoy a sense of the sea with this straw bag displaying creatures in the bubbling pearl water. *Courtesy of Anne Hopkin.*

Green suede handbag with folding closure, brass turning clasp and single strap handle, labeled "Marlow, made in USA." 9" x 5.5". *Courtesy of Piacente*

Handbag of beige silk with matching "Holiday" fine shoes. *Courtesy of Steppin' Out.*

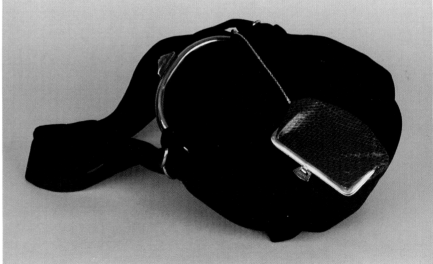

Black wool bag by Lewis with red lizard interior. 10" h. (shown open and closed). *Courtesy of Steppin' Out.*

Brown cordé handbag, the tag is unreadable. 10'' x 9''. *Courtesy of Steppin' Out.*

Two purses by 66 Berger Bags. Left: black silk clutch with grey metal clasp bar. 10.5'' long. Right: black leather round box bag with plastic bands and handle and red leather interior. 5.25'' dia. x 6'' h. *Courtesy of Steppin' Out.*

Primera Roma Magazine handbag. *Courtesy of Peggy Ann Osborne.*

Magazine handbag, Italian. 4.5'' x 12''. *Courtesy of Katy Kane.*

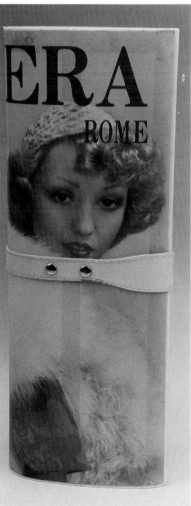

Embroidered leather with gold finish, brass frame with aqua enameled catch. Embroidery in metallic and silk threads of Oriental figures. *Courtesy of Steppin' Out.*

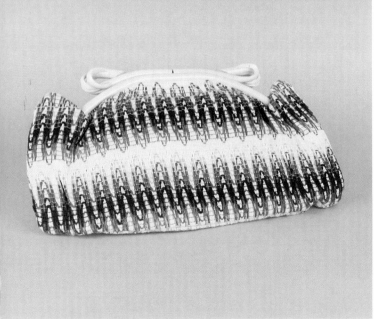

Colorful cloth clutch with ivory colored plastic frame and catch. 14.5" x 8.25". *Courtesy of Steppin' Out.*

Black suede bag with pierced metal top and brass frame. Signed "Magro Original." 6.5" x 8". *Courtesy of Steppin' Out.*

Plain, purple cloth bag and hat by "Arlington Hats." 10.5" x 9.5". *Courtesy of Steppin' Out.*

Pink and grey striped hat and drawstring bag by Sherman Saint Louis. *Courtesy of Steppin' Out.*

Four clutch bags with soft bow designed flaps. (Back left) pink ribbed silk, unmarked. (Back right) red leather and white cotton cloth, unmarked. (Front) two suede, purple and aqua marked Mardlay. *Courtesy of Steppin' Out.*

Brown kid bag of kidney shape with two strap handles, mirror fixed under the lid, 9.5'' x 4.5''. *Courtesy of Piacente*

1950s brown leather handbag marked Duchess. Architectural style. 14.25'' x 13.75''. *Courtesy of Steppin' Out.*

Knitted brown and black diagonal pattern signed Lucien Lelong. Silk lining, brass frame and catch with black round dots and half pearls. 10.25'' x 7''. *Courtesy of Steppin' Out.*

Black suede with two brass bars and looped handle signed Hattie Carnegie. Has interior hand mirror and change purse. 9'' x 12''. *Courtesy of Steppin' Out.*

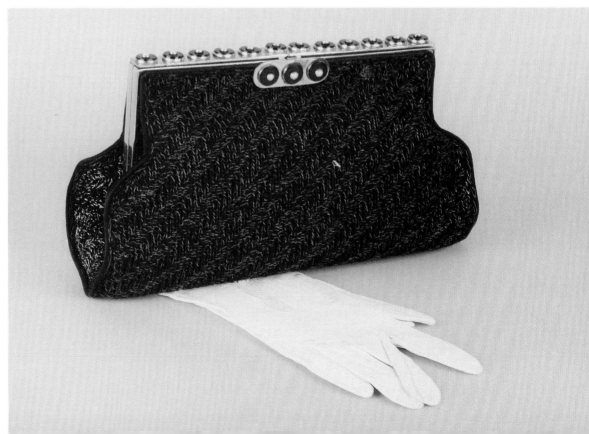

Black silk clutch with gold and silver embroidered flap. Signed "Milch Bag." 12" x 9.5". *Courtesy of Steppin' Out.*

Two beaded clutch bags of particularly small, close beadwork. *Courtesy of Piacente*

Grey suede handbag with black plastic frame and two silver lines, suede handle. Signed Harry Rosenfeld Original. Change purse, mirror and comb inside. 8" x 10". *Courtesy of Steppin' Out.*

Hand warmer of black and woven wool, silk lined with zippered compartment. 17" x 8". *Courtesy of Steppin' Out.*

Two bags with plastic: (left) white squares marked "Original Carmello Squares by Saks Fifth Avenue." 13" x 11.5". (right) strips of colored ribbed plastic laced together. Plaxtic rolls, by Jolles Corp., USA. 12" x 7.5". *Courtesy of Steppin' Out.*

Two clutch bags with white laces joining pierc
plastic tiles. Made by Plasticflex. *Courtesy of
Steppin' Out.*

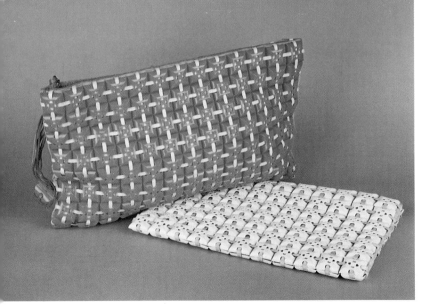

Another blue "caviar bag" from the early
1950s. *Courtesy of Classics Illustrated,
William Goldberg.*

Four "telephone wire" handbags in
primary colors, all unmarked, c. 1950s.
Courtesy of Steppin' Out.

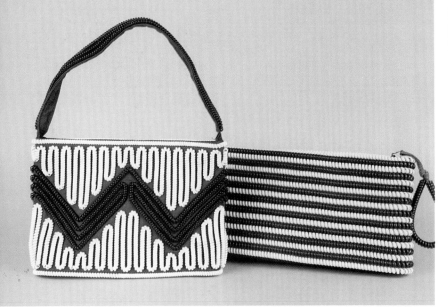

Two "telephone wire" handbags,
unmarked, c. 1950s. *Courtesy of Steppin'
Out.*

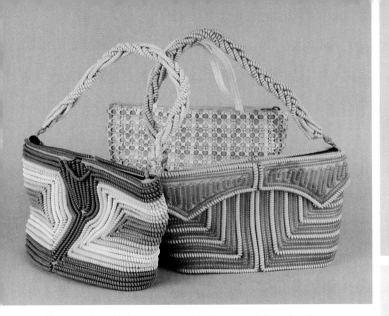

Three plastic bags, two in front with telephone wire and one in back with plastic loops. *Courtesy of Steppin' Out.*

Blue calf accordion bag with white dotted lining. *Courtesy of Rover and Lorber*

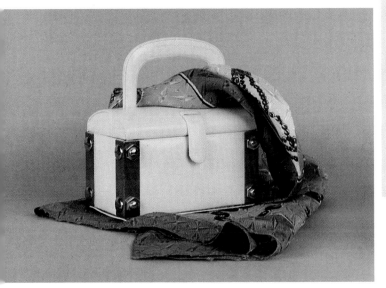

White calf bag with gold trim on the corners. *Courtesy of Steppin' Out.*

Black lizard and white ostrich leather bags marked "Deutz". Leather lined. 8" x 4.5". *Courtesy of Radio Times.*

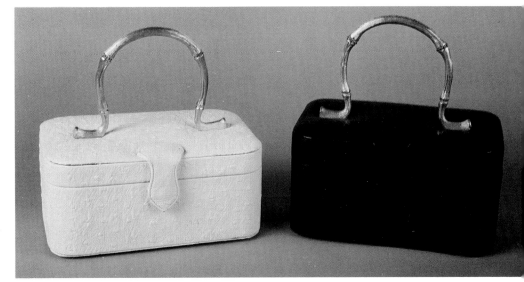

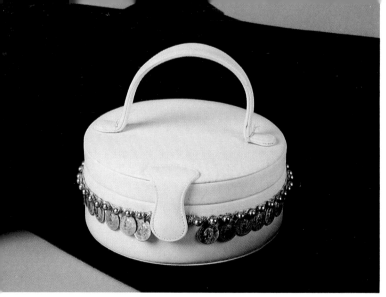

White leather bag trimmed with gold coins. 6.5" d. x 3" h. *Courtesy of Radio Times.*

Black calf bag with coins and gimp trim. Made by Deutz. 6.5" x 3.5". *Courtesy of Radio Times.*

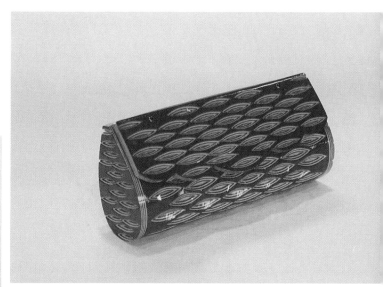

Orange overlay cut through plastic clutch. *Courtesy of Rover and Lorber*

"Caviar bag." Fre-Mor Original, c. 1950s. 5.75" x 7.5". *Courtesy of Kaylee Freedman.*

Black alligator box bag by Deutz. *Courtesy of Radio Times.*

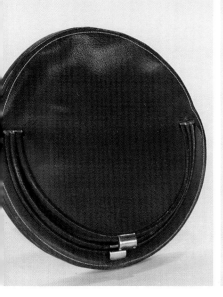

Brown pigskin leather clutch expanding to provide two compartments. Marked "Abercrombie & Fitch Co. N.Y." "Made in Austria." 10" diameter. *Courtesy of Steppin' Out.*

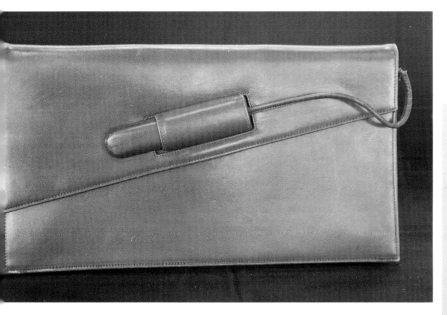

Brown leather clutch with green leather interior by Lederer de Paris. 13.5" x 7.5". *Courtesy of Rover and Lorber*

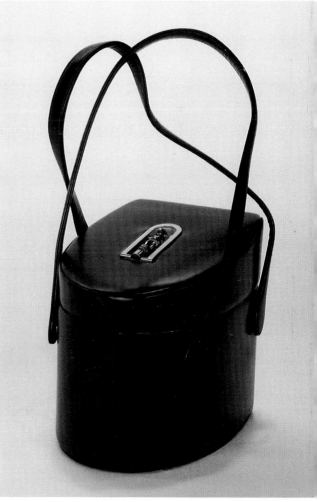

Blue calf bag in oval shape by Rosenfeld. The lid displays a swivel statue. Made in France. 6" x 5". *Courtesy of Rover and Lorber*

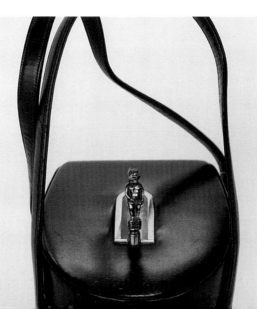

Gold lamé clutch bag with clear plastic exterior, rhinestone studded frame with clasp, and interior matching change purse, labeled "Exclusive Faye Mell Design, Fleurette, Inc., Miami, Fla.," 14" x 7".
Courtesy of Piacente

Cream leather with two carved horsehead ends and jockey cap clasp. Signed Rosenfeld.
Courtesy of Rover and Lorber

Bakelite clasp on a tapestry bag. 7'' x 10.25''.
Courtesy of Francine Cohen.

Two gold beaded bags. The
bag on the left is trimmed in
brass and marked Tyrolean.
The bag on the right is
unmarked. *Courtesy of
Rovere and Lorber.*

Black beaded bag. *Courtesy of Anne
Hopkin.*

Dark blue beaded bags by Quaker. Wonoco Yarn
Co., NY, c. 1947. *Courtesy of Steppin' Out.*

1940s brown and black beaded bags by Wonoco.
Courtesy of Steppin' Out.

Chapter 5

1960s—The Hippie Years

The 1960s were a decade of controversy over such issues as Vietnam, civil rights and personal freedom. Worldwide, the influences of popular music including the Beatles, the Rolling Stones and folk music emerged to question old standards and encourage individual thinking. In America, John F. Kennedy was elected President in 1960 with a platform of youth, energy and high hopes.

As the First Lady, his wife Jacqueline influenced fashion toward the elegant, restrained styles of fine tailoring and high-quality workmanship. Throughout the early sixties, sleek classic handbags of formal designs used calf and alligator leather, fine beadwork and metal.

Later in the decade, as the Vietnam conflict grew into a war under Presidents Johnson and Nixon, young and restless people protested America's involvement. In step with the popular and political climate, womens' fashion evolved from predominantly ladylike tailoring to blue jeans, sweatshirts and country-casual styles. Handbags were big, and the skirts were short—very short in the late sixties.

Early Judith Leiber handbag made of blue calfskin with half circle handle and brass ribbed grips, c. late-1960s. 9.75" x 8". *Courtesy of Steppin' Out.*

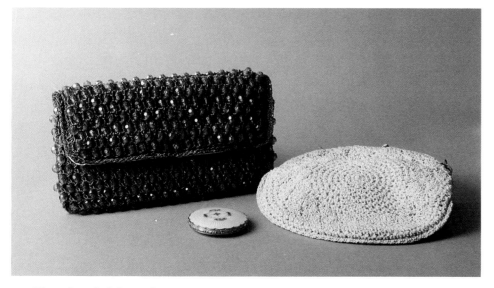

Two beaded bags from the 1960s. *Courtesy of Anne Hopkin.*

Handbag styles reflected the shift to individualistic shapes and materials including woven baskets, soft crush leathers, personalized tooling or monograms, and even decoupage lunchboxes! In the name of individuality, a shift was made from haut couture styling to homemade fashions that allowed anyone and everyone to "do their own thing." Moreover, the general populace began to prefer simpler, more mundane and less costly fashions, so many design houses lost their influence and their clientele. By the end of the decade, bags were often as homemade and freeform as the attitudes of the day.

Handbag and folding handle both covered with silver beads with covered frame and silver clasp, 7.5" x 4.25". Oval box-type handbag covered with brown beads, with a sliding lid and strap handle, 9" x 4.5". Small bag covered with dark blue iridescent beads, zippered closure and two matching handles, 8.5" x 4.5". *Courtesy of Piacente*

Red alligator bag, c. 1960s, with the strap attached to the front and back. 10" x 7.5". *Courtesy of Kaylee Freedman.*

Gold bag with upright handle by Bienes-Davis. 5.5" x 9".

Large black alligator bag marked Sterling USA, c. 1960s. 14" x 10". *Courtesy of Kaylee Freedman.*

Blue ribbed silk, rectangular clutch with sliding catch with brass end engraved "MCB" signed Elizabeth Arden. 9.5" x 6.5". *Courtesy of Steppin' Out.*

Black beaded bag with metal trim. 7.5" x 4".
Courtesy of Peggy Ann Osborne.

Imitation of the Gucci bamboo handle bag. Maker
unknown, c. 1960s. *Courtesy of Classics Illustrated,
William Goldberg.*

Blue felt bag with gold leaf clasp, not marked, 5.5"
x 8".

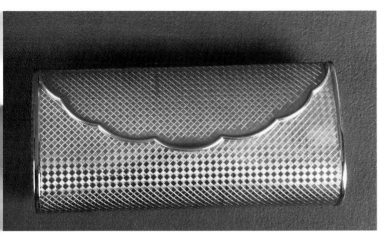

Gold metal bag with mirror on inside of lid.

White skin bag by Etra, c. 1960s. 6" x 9". *Courtesy of Classics Illustrated, William Goldberg.*

Black wool bag by Ingberg, c. 1960s. 10" x 10". *Courtesy of Classics Illustrated, William Goldberg.*

Black lizard bag, maker unknown, c. 1960s. 9" x 12". *Courtesy of Classics Illustrated, William Goldberg.*

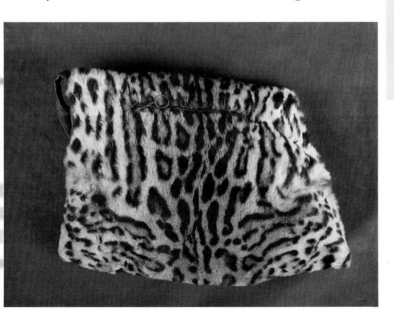

Leopard bag.

Straw bag with mouse figures playing cards,
signed "Nan, Box 235, Buck Hill Falls, PA."
Mirror inside. 8.5 " (to mice) x 6" sq.

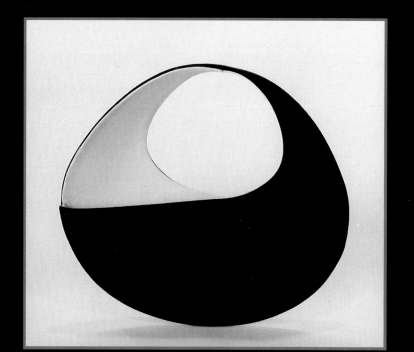

Leather American Indian style bag with initials
R.B. Robin marked on back. Silver belt, tip and
clasp. 14" x 14" x 5". *Courtesy of Mim Klein.*

Two saddle bag designs: brown suede, unmarked.
11.5" x 14"; black and tan bag by Walker Western,
Wickenburg, Arizona. *Courtesy of Steppin' Out.*

Ingberg handbag from c. 1960. 6" x 9". *Courtesy of Classics Illustrated, William Goldberg.*

Lunch box bag made in the 1960s. Very popular at the time, these were handmade bags considered quite the fashion. *Courtesy of Barbara Dollaway Michie.*

Red leather bag with two strap handles and zippered closure marked "Coach, ... No. 0533-020," 13.5" x 12.5".

Light brown leather duffle bag with two outside change purses by Coach. 12" x 5.5". *Courtesy of Steppin' Out.*

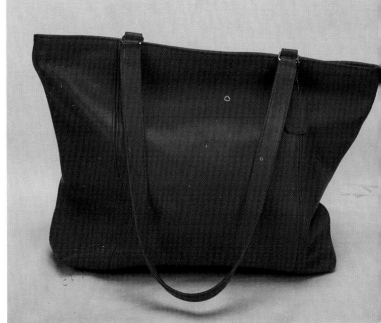

Chapter 6

1970s and 1980s—Designer Years

The 1970s had its share of social and political turbulence as a spill-over from the late 1960s. Society struggled with the ramifications of the '60s "sexual revolution," with more civil rights difficulties, and with further changes in the role of women in the home and at work. As debacle (Watergate) followed disaster (Vietnam), many citizens grew increasingly disillusioned with the American government.

In this disarray, it is no surprise that 1970s fashions were also a jumble. Designs borrowed from the forties (like platform and wingtip shoes) were mixed with pop-art presentation in bold colors and patterns. Sports-related styles made big inroads to popular taste, and the fashion designers made their own sportswear lines, since formal wear was out of fashion. Because no clear direction emerged in seventies fashion, a variety of playful styles developed, including comic characters, toy-line images, and generally unsophisticated designs.

Black and white striped canvas half-round bag with single black woven strap labeled "Milano Series, Line Exchange, 1 Sulgrave Road, Scarsdale, N.Y., Domus Products, Chase Bag Company, Reidsville, North Carolina," 22" x 12".

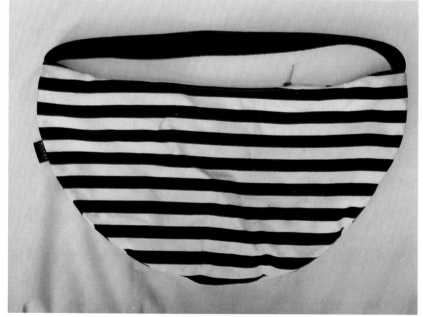

Striped, "Made in Italy by Roberta DiCamerino" with key to lock, 11.5" h. (with handle up) x 8.5" x 4".

Perhaps in an effort to establish *something* with an undisputedly high fashion value, the public began to support those designers whose items were identified with a bold, recognizable logo. Some of the most collectible handbags of this "designer" era are the so-called "status bags"—handbags considered fashionable because the designer's name is prominently displayed on the body of the bag. A far cry from the homespun approach of the preceding decade, the collectible bags from the '70s come from the biggest of the "big-name" handbag designers—from Gucci, Louis Vuitton, Fendi and a few select others. This trend was to continue into the 1980s as well.

Red and white striped canvas bag with woven red strap handles and zippered closure labeled "Fine Canvas, Accessories Unlimited of Maine, Cornish, ME 04020," 12" x 10".

Black and white striped cloth bag with zippered top closure and black leather-like trim and two strap handles, 21" x 12", and a separate matching zippered clutch, 9" x 7".

Leather handbag with initials, the "preppy" look.

Straw bag by Etienne Aignér

Nantucket lightship basket with oval scrimshaw top panel, all hand-made.

Straw bags: Left: Leurs, Right: Koret.

Two quilted Souleiado cloth bags with two long strap handles and zipper closure labeled "Wald-come, Made in France," Left: red, 12" x 8". Right: black, 11" x 9".

Quilted cloth shoulder bag with two strap handles and duffle bag shape with zipper closure labeled "Vera Bradley, Indiana," 12" x 6".

Blue wool Bargello needlework bag with zipper closure and double wool rope handles, made by M. B. Schiffer, 14" x 10.5".

Quilted cloth shoulder bag with top zipper closure, 13" x 9".

Gold-plated purse with paste accents of a woman and the outline of her dog. Marked "Miriam Marshall" c. 1980s. *Courtesy of Francine Cohen.*

Black textured bag with red leather base, trim and handles labeled "Longchamp" and zippered closure, 16.5" x 12".

Beaded American Indian cloth bag designed with three roses. Unmarked. 14.25" x 12.5". *Courtesy of Mim Klein.*

A modern design from the 1970s, red leather. 9" x 14". *Courtesy of Francine Cohen.*

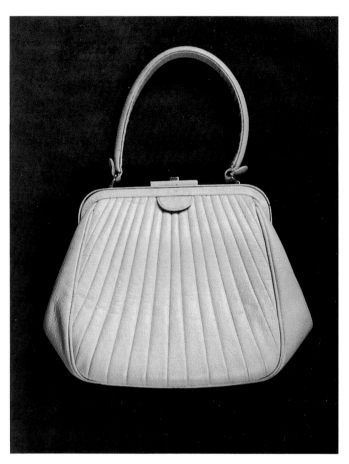

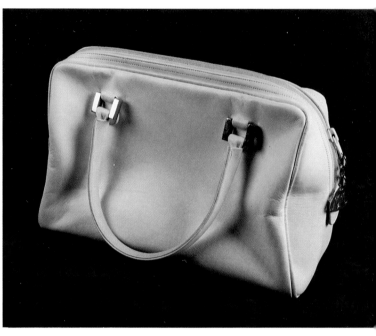

White leather handbag by Morris Moskowitz.

Creme leather bag of kidskin by Koret.

Red wooden handbag by Lady London Inc., c. 1970s. Felt lined inside. 5.5" x 10". *Courtesy of Classics Illustrated, William Goldberg.*

Black and white striped canvas bag with white woven strap handles and six brass snap closures labeled "The Americana Collection by Accessories Unlimited, ... in Cornish, Me. U.S.A.," 16" x 14".

Green canvas bag with two strap handles and an outside pocket decorated with the image of a pig, and two interior plastic pockets with zippered closures, 15" x 15".

Leather purse made in Italy expressly for Bloomingdales Department Store, c. 1970s. 4.5" x 9". *Courtesy of Francine Cohen.*

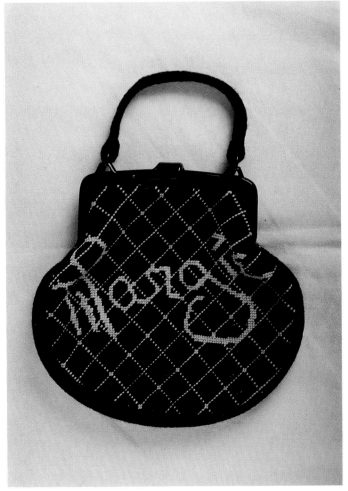

Various needlepoint bags.

Green leather bag, c. 1970s. Maker unknown.

"Preppy" vinyl bag, c. early-1980s.

Colorful needlepoint bag.

Gucci

Gucci was founded in Florence, Italy in 1922 by Guccio Gucci with a staff of craftsmen whose families had been leatherworkers for generations. It began as a saddlery, producing handcrafted leather goods; without much difficulty, they began producing fashionable handbags as well and the company went international. They prospered greatly in the '50s, '60s, and early '70s, acquiring status tantamount to companies that had been in the industry for over a century.

In the '80s, the company grew at an exhorbinant rate. Gucci bags were available everywhere, and the company became known for the double-G logo that appeared on a wide range of their products. Still, this new, broader market had its drawbacks. The counterfeit market went wild with the Gucci logo, and the company began to lose some of its credibility.

Gucci is probably most known for its trend-setting bamboo handled bag, created in 1957. Their hobo shoulder bag, removed from the market in 1975, was revised and placed back in stores in 1991.

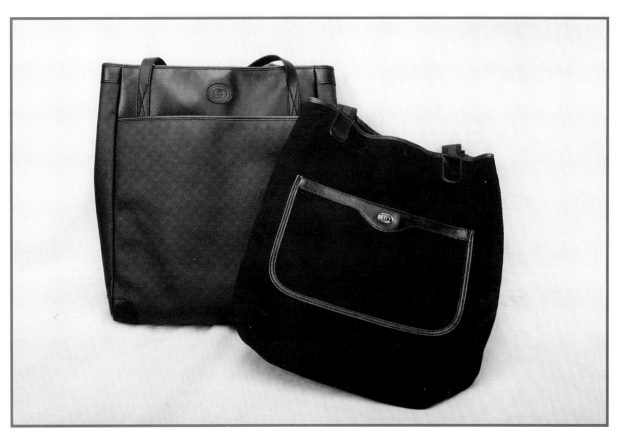

Two black Gucci bags. Left: two strap handles and one outside pocket marked "Gucci, Made in Italy," with black leather and patterned black treated leather-like material stamped with overall black linked GG logos of Gucci, 13" x 16". Right: cloth bag with woven green and red cloth strap handles and an outside pocket, marked "GUCCI Accessory Collection, Made in Italy," 16" x 14".

Travel bag of blue silk with reversible cover in blue suede and calf by Gucci. 8.5" x 6.25".
Courtesy of Steppin' Out.

Brown leather Gucci bag.

The bamboo handle Gucci bag first introduced by Gucci in 1957.

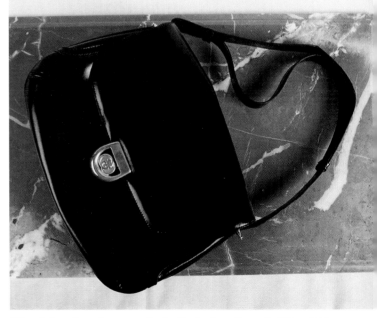

Black leather bag made in Italy by Gucci. 9" x 11".

Pierre Deux

The Pierre Deux antique furniture shop opened in 1967 on Bleeker Street in New York City, under the ownership of Pierre Moulin and Pierre Le Vec—thus the name "the two Pierres." Ironically, they soon found that the patrons of the shop were more interested in the Souleiado fabric decorating the shop than they were in the actual antiques! In the early 1970s, Pierre Deux introduced handbags to its line, made, of course, from the fabric that was to make their fortune.

Souleiado, an old Provencal word meaning "the sun's rays shining through a cloud after the rain," describes the colorful and cheerful cotton fabric that has been made since the 17th century in Tarascon, France. It can be traced back to the Phoenicians who settled in present-day Marseilles to make "painted fabrics. During the industrial revolution, when traditional craftsmanship was lost to heavy machinery in many companies, Souleiado fabrics were printed by hand with carved fruitwood blocks, just as they always had been. Now, new designs are created only by taking elements from the original patterns in combination with one another, thereby maintaining the authenticity of the fabric's prints.

Three Pierre Deux bags. Left to right: blue quilted cloth bag with two strap handles, side pocket and Velcro closure labeled "Souleiado, fabriqué en France," 12" x 14"; blue quilted cloth duffle bag with zippered closure labeled "La Provence de Pierre Deux, Souleiado, hand made," 12.5" x 6"; green quilted cloth bag with covered roping handles and zipper closure labeled "Souleiado, fabriqué en France," 18" x 13".

Various Pierre Deux bags. *Courtesy of Pierre Deux.*

Louis Vuitton

In 1852, Louis Vuitton was the exclusive luggage maker for Empress Eugenie, the wife of Napoleon III. In 1854 Vuitton established his own Paris trunk-maker shop, and introduced flat trunks which could be easily stacked for travel by train or ship. In 1892, Louis Vuitton began making handbags as well, and in 1896 his son Georges Vuitton created the LV stamped canvas that is so well-known today.

Handbag in Louis Vuitton logo print with flat base, single curved handle and folded flap secured with a brass hinged clasp, 12'' x 8''.

Handbag with two short strap handles in Louis Vuitton logo print, flat oval base, 9.5''.

Three pockets, the center one with zippered closure and interior compartments, two short strap handles in Louis Vuitton logo print, 12'' x 8''.

Duffle bag with shoulder strap in Louis Vuitton logo print with top zipper, outside pocket with flap closure, and two grip side handles, 18'' x 12''.

Shoulder bag with top zipper in Louis Vuitton logo print, 10'' x 6''.

New Louis Vuitton bag.

Shoulder bag with single belted strap marked "LOUIS VUITTON, PARIS, made in France," with top zipper, 20'' x 14''.

Advertisement for Louis Vuitton bags in 1903.

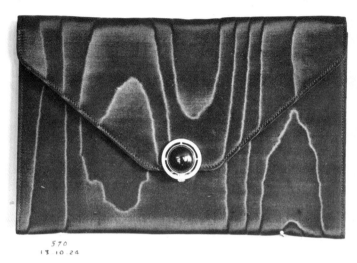

Louis Vuitton clutch bag from 1924.

In 1910, this bag was advertised as "the shopping bag." *Courtesy of Louis Vuitton.*

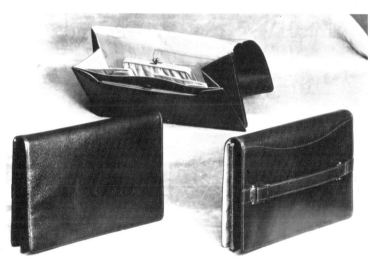

Advertised as the "Ambassadeur" bag in the 1930s by Louis Vuitton.

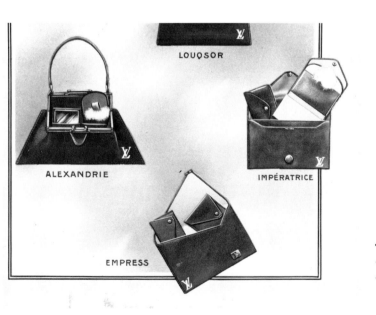

Three bags by Louis Vuitton in 1910, the "Alexandrie," the "Impératrice," and the "Empress."

143

Clutch pocketbooks from the 1930s.

This cowhide bag was advertised as the "sac à ouvrages," the working bag, in 1936.

34066

Handbags of cowhide and patent leather. *Courtesy of Louis Vuitton.*

Judith Leiber

Judith Leiber was born in Budapest, Hungary, where she was apprenticed to the Hungarian Handbag Guild and became the first woman of the Guild to achieve the rank of "master." When she moved to the United States in 1947 she worked as a designer for a large, mass market handbag manufacturer, until the poor quality and craftmanship led her to open her own company in 1963. She now produces some of the finest quality bags in the world. They are carried to inaugurations and other international diplomatic and society affairs, and are displayed in many major museums, including the Smithsonian and the Metropolitan Museum of Art.

Leiber is known mostly for her unique, animal-shaped minaudières, delicately decorated with tiny rhinestones of different colors. Judith Leiber bags span a wide spectrum of styles, however —from her famous beaded and jeweled bags to beautiful skin bags of various colors and forms. She says she finds inspiration for the design in almost everything— "in architecture, in dresses and furniture, paintings." Her fine frames and clasps, with their lovely jeweled details, bring to mind the great jewelry names of the '20s and '30s, Boucheron, Bulgari, Cartier and Boisvin.

Wonderful advertisements for the Judith Leiber bags putting the bags in their native environment.

Judith Leiber

Handbags/ Accessories

Judith Leiber

Handbags/ Accessories

Judith Leiber 1986 ©

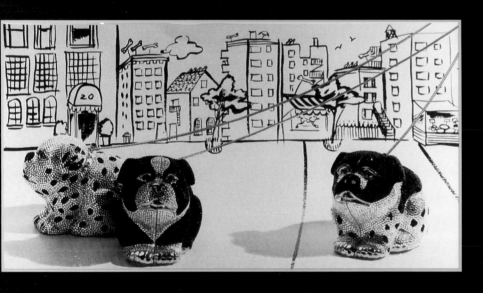

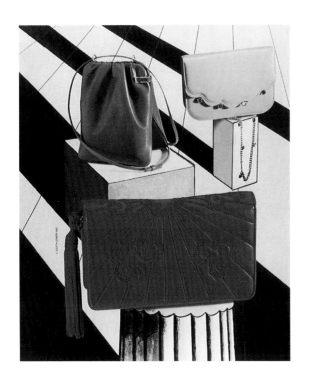

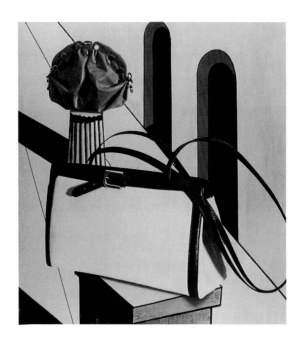

The exquisite detail and design are evident on
these bags. *Courtesy of Judith Leiber Handbags
and Accessories.*

Skin bags from Judith Leiber are also very popular
and have gorgeous clasps and bars.

Bibliography

Haertig, Evelyn. *Antique Combs and Purses*. Carmel, Calif.: Gallery Graphics Press, 1983.

Peltz, Leslie Ruth. *Fashion Accessories*. 2nd Ed. Indianapolis, Indiana: The Bobbs-Merrill Company, 1980.

Love, Harriet. *Harriet Love's Guide to Vintage Chic*. New York: Holt, Rinehart and Winston, 1982.

Prisco, Dorothy D., Ed.D, and Harold W. Moore, Ed.D. *Fashion Merchandise Information*. New York: John Wiley & Sons, 1986.

The New York Times, Sunday, October 23, 1988 "Boxy Bags Full of Memories."

Ettinger, Roseann. *Handbags*. West Chester, Pennsylvania: Schiffer Publishing, Ltd., 1991.

Index

Price Guide

Prices in this guide indicate a range of values, dependent on many factors. These can include the condition of the item, the type of shop, and the vagarities of an ever-changing market. Designer and manufacturer names can also be a factor, as can the lining (vinyl or glove-soft kidskin) and fittings (frames and clasps of silver, brass, Bakelite etc.) Prices of alligator and crocodile bags vary particularly widely, based on the quality and the condition of the skins; baby alligator skin is considered especially fine. This listing is intended to provide today's handbag enthusiasts with a general idea of relative values. All prices are given in U.S. dollars.

page	bag	price range
5	Bargello	$ 400-500
6	Bargello	400-500
	Alligator	50-250
7	Alligator	special
	Alligator/Felt	25-150
	Art Nouveau	100-140
	Leather (Basco)	95-125
8	Japanese	300-400
9	Ortega	75-110
10	Ortega (top)	75-110
	Chimayo	65-95
	Architectural	125-200 ea.
11	ETL	65-120
	Clutch (right)	75-120
12	Van Cleef & Arpels	350-450
	Silhouette	300-400
13	Leather/Plastic	300-400
	Tapestry (left)	300-375
	Tapestry (right)	300-375
14	Mesh (top)	100-175
	Mesh (bottom)	65-95 ea.
16	Anton Moritz	400-500
	Carnegie	250-350
	Onyx Clasp	275-376
17	Art Nouveau	200-275
	Marcasite	250-350
	Plique-à-jour	300-400
	Beaded	200-265
18	Tortoise shell	1600-1850
	Tapestry	850-950
	Mesh	95-175
19	Sax-Kay	250-350
	Bergdorf Goodman	375-475
	Oriental Bakelite	295-375
20	Embroidered	300-400
	Lizard	200-275
21	Leather/Reptile	200-275
	Deco/German silver	150-250
	Glass stones/beads	265-300
22	Rhinestones	125-225
	Paste, Chrysoprase...	275-375

page	bag	price range
	Enamel	225-300
23	Minaudières	175-275 ea.
24	Gold/Purple	265-400
	Lady & Knight	300-425
25	Red Bakelite	195-250
	B/W Enamel	85-140
26	Tasselled (top)	200-300 ea.
	Enamel (bottom)	140-200
27	Enamel (top left)	300-400
	Metal/Blue Beads	75-150
	Kit bag	75-125
	Beaded Peacock	225-300
28	Beaded Pouch	95-125
	Ada Grunfeld	200-325
	Deco Beaded	200-325
	Beaded Mesh	100-200
29	Plastic Frame	90-130
	Floral Beaded	150-250
	Knitted/Beaded	95-140
	Deco Beaded	200-375
30	Bronze Beaded	65-100
	Beaded Peacock	75-110
	Pouch style	250-350
31	Velvet	200-285
	Beaded/Cameo	95-150
	Victorian String	85-130
32	Victorian Pouches	125-200 ea.
33	Suede/Enamel	95-125
	Two Suede Bags	200-295 ea.
34	Brown Suede	90-130
	Black Suede	90-130
	Mark Cross	100-150
35	Cornelian Clasp	95-150
	Petit Point	65-120
	Deco enamel	90-175
	Silk	75-100
36	Black Suede	80-150
	Pouch/Bakelite	90-125
	Leather/Locusts	195-300
	Green Silk	200-325
37	Bakelite, Deco (top)	300-400

	Bakelite (middle)	250-325
	Bakelite, Deco (bottom)	250-350
38	Art Deco	120-200
	Gold Metal Casing	200-325
	"Fruit Salad"	200-325
39	Oriental Fan shape	225-300
	Needlepoint	125-200
	Oriental Frame	90-125
40	Art Deco Reticule	195-275
41	Chalcedony	225-325
	Normandy	225-300
	Beaded Deco	100-150
42	Beaded Deco	120-200
43	Black Satin	75-140
	Gold/Mother of Pearl	80-110
	Beaded, Bonwit Teller	125-200
44	Art Deco, cloth	250-350
	Bakelite	95-125
	Art Deco, Bakelite	90-140
45	Black Beaded	40-75
46	Suede/Lamé	35-60
	Black Bag	55-70
	Green Bakelite	100-140
	Black Bag w/purse	55-70
47	Green Leather	60-95
	Brown Suede	8-45
48	Leather	75-100
	Long Clutch	65-100
49	Brown Felt	60-95
	Black Calf	120-175 ea.
50	Low Drum Shape	295-400
	Accordian	300-400
	Tall Drum Shape	200-300
	Marcasite bag	75-110
51	Gold Leather	5-25
	Black Satin	10-65
	Cloth w/Gold Trim	75-200
52	Cloth/Cupids	75-125
	Tooled Leather	40-65
	Lavendar Liberty	50-75
53	Black Kid	15-65
	Black Wool	10-45
	Embroidered Silk	65-90
54	Black Suede	20-125
55	Blue Suede	15-55
	Black Suede Clutch	8-35
56	Brown Cordé	75=120
	Pony Skin	25-45 ea.
	Expandable	60-95 ea.
	Mexican	25-45 ea.
57	Blue Kid (top)	60-90
	Red Kid (top)	60-90
	Black Wool (top)	75-100
	Red Kid w/Strap	10-35
	Red Kid Clutch	15-150
58	"Lewis" Wool	10-65
	Brown Suede	20-100
	Plastic	25-45
59	Silver Leather	40-75
	Blue Calf	70-95
	Plastic Tile	25-45 ea.
60	Petit Point	75-110
	Red Leather Clutch	45-70
	Red Leather Roll	40-60
61	Box Bags	120-200 ea.
	Red Alligator "ship"	225-300
	Argentinian Alligator	200-275
73	"Deitsch" Alligator	15-85
77	Triangular Alligator	20-150
	Rectangular Alligator	35-125
	Alligator w/plastic	20-150
78	Small Alligator	Rare; No price available
	Green Alligator Clutch	30-150
79	Alligator Envelope	45-175
	Red Alligator Shoulder	35-175
	Faux Alligator	40-150
80	Alligator (center)	35-165
	Alligator (bottom)	35-175
81	Red Crocodile Clutch	40-150
	Brown Alligator	45-185
	Alligator Claw Wallet	Hard to find; no value available
82	Alligator Dressing Kit	50-100
	Blue Alligator	Very unusual color, shape; no value available
83	Belle Alligator	25-150
	Paper Fan	Rare; no value available
	Rectangular Alligator	35-150
85	Green Alligator	Very rare, unusual shape; no value available
86	Alligator Pouch	25-85
	Brown Suede	8-45
	Red Alligator	35-150
	Brown Pieced Alligator	10-75
87	"Edith Uffner"	45-125
	Two-tone Alligator	20-150
	Small "boat" Alligator	20-85
	Tall alligator	25-150
88	Brown Alligator	35-125
	Alligator Jewelry Case	Hard to find; 25-150
	Alligator (bottom left)	45-150
	Alligator (bottom right)	45-175

89	Pin & Earrings	Very hard to find; no value available
91	Walrus Skin	15-150
	Alligator (head & feet)	25-85
92	Brown Suede & lizard	12-30
	Two Leather Clutches	8-45
93	Dorset-Rex Plastic Bag	100-200
	Tyrolean Plastic Bag	17-225
94	Plastic, Pail Shape	100-150
	Lewsid Jewels	120-170 ea.
95	Wilardy Brown Plastic	100-150
	Ivory Plastic Bag	125-160
	Gray Plastic & Metal	100-150
	Plastic w/Rhinestones	100-150
	"Coffin" Plastic Bag	120-175
96	"Henryfrank" Plastic	100-140
	Black Plastic	120-160
	Gray Half-circle	75-120
97	Leather w/Metal	75-100
98	Aluminum (silver color)	90-120
	Aluminum (gold color)	110-140
	Clear Vinyl	40-70
	Straw	65-110
99	Clear Vinyl w/Gold	75-100
	Vinyl w/Silver Frame	60-100
	Emilio Pucci	300-400
	Horse & Elephant	110-185
100	Black Calf Leather	65-95
	Wicker & Felt	45-75
	Gold Lamé Bag	80-110
	White Beaded Bag	55-85
101	Gold Leather Clutch	95-125
	Three Metal Baskets	75-135 ea.
102	Bulldog	175-250
	Straw w/Fruit	40-75
	Accordian-top Bag	150-200
	Martin Clutch	35-60
	Book Bag (blue)	90-110
	Book Bag (brown)	70-95
103	Leopard Handwarmer	150-225
	Navy & Ecru	95-120
	Brown & Amber	75-110
	Black w/Bees	70-110
104	Fortuny	100-150
	Black Suede	75-110
	Black Satin	65-100
	Tooled Leather (left)	45-90
	Tooled Leather (center)	35-70
	Tooled Leather (right)	90-145
105	Cotton on Gold Frame	60-90
	Ivory w/Floral	70-100
	Leopard Skin	75-100
	Straw & Pearls	40-75
106	Beige Silk	60-100
	Black Wool	75-100
107	Brown Cordé	75-110
	Primera Roma	75-95

	Magazine Handbag	75-95
	Embroidered Leather	150-200
108	Cloth Clutch	55-85
	Black Suede	70-110
	Pink & Gray Stripes	60-90
	Purple Cloth	85-100
109	Four Clutch Bags	55-85 ea.
	Brown Kid Bag	10-45
	Brown Leather	70-120
110	Knitted Brown & Black	150-200
	Black Suede	120-185
111	Black Embroidered Silk	75-100
	Grey Suede	80-120
	Two bags (center left)	50-70 ea.
	Handwarmer	40-60
	Two Plastic Bags	40-75
112	Plastic Tile Clutches	45-70 ea.
	Blue Caviar Bag	85-100
	4 Telephone Wire Bags	65-95 ea.
	2 Telephone Wire Bags	60-90 ea.
113	2 Telephone Wire Bags	65-95
	Plastic Loop Bag	40-70
	White Calf	85-120
	Blue Calf Accordian	120-200
	White Ostrich	120-160
	Black Lizard	150-200
114	White Leather w/Coins	85-130
	Black Calf w/Coins	95-150
	Caviar Bag	60-90
	Orange Overlay	250-350
	Black Alligator	160-200
115	Brown Pigskin	120-200
	Brown Leather Clutch	125-175
	Blue Calf	200-250
116	Gold Lamé	5-15
	Cream Leather	225-285
117	Tapestry	70-95
	Tyrolean (center left)	100-150
	Beaded (center right)	55-80
	Beaded Bag (bottom)	50-75
118	Blue Beaded Bags	40-75 ea.
	Wonoco Beaded Bags	40-75 ea.
119	Early Judith Leiber	200-300
	Two Beaded Bags	35-55 ea.
120	Handled Beaded Bag	15-65
	Beaded Bag (left)	15-65
	Beaded Bag (right)	10-35
121	Red Alligator	200-250
	Gold Bag	75-95
	Alligator, "Sterling"	125-200
	Blue Ribbed Silk	70-95
122	Black Beaded Bag	65-90
	Blue Felt	80-110
	Imitation Gucci	45-85
123	Gold Metal Bag	50-70
	Black Wool, Ingberg	55-80
	White Skin Bag	45-70
	Black Lizard	100-160
	Leopard Bag	50-75

124	Straw Mouse Bag	85-110
	B/W Geometric Bag	200-300
125	Indian-style Leather	150-200
	Saddle Bag Designs	85-110 ea.
126	Ingberg Bag	40-65
	Lunchbox Bag	45-75
	Leather Duffle	95-120
	Red Leather, "Coach"	100-130
127	B/W Striped Canvas	35-60
	DiCamerino, w/Key	75-100
128	Red & White Striped	35-60
	B/W Striped Cloth	55-90
	Leather "Preppy" Bag	100-120
129	Aignér Straw Bag	50-75
	Nantucket Lightship	700-1000
	Straw Basket (left)	40-65
	Straw Basket (right)	30-55
130	Two Quilted Bags	75-95 ea.
	Quilted (two handles)	90-130
	Blue Wool Bargello	200-300
	Quilted (one strap)	75-95
	Gold-plated w/Silhouette	200-300
131	Beaded American Indian	300-400
	Black w/Red Base	200-300
	Red Leather	250-350
132	Cream Leather Kidskin	200-250
	Moskowitz White	100-150
	Red Wooden	75-100
133	Green Canvas w/Pig	45-70
	B/W Striped Canvas	55-75
	Bloomingdales Leather	150-200
134	Various Needlepoint	175-225 ea.
135	Preppy Vinyl	60-80
	Green Leather	50-85
	Needlepoint	100-125
136	Gucci (left)	230-300
	Gucci (right)	200-275
137	Brown Gucci	265-300
	Gucci Blue Silk	150-200
	Bamboo Gucci	225-300
	Black Leather Gucci	250-300
138	Pierre Deux	75-120 ea.
140	Louis Vuitton	375-425
141	Louis Vuitton 3-pocket	275-300
	Louis Vuitton w/2 Short Straps	200-275
	Louis Vuitton Duffle	125-200
142	Louis Vuitton Shoulder	200-275
	New Louis Vuitton	350-450
	Louis Vuitton, Belted Strap	225-300